THE TECHNICAL WRITER'S GUIDE

WITH EXERCISES

Alma G. Bryant

University of South Florida - Tampa

Jane H. Duke

University of South Florida - Tampa

Kendall/Hunt
Publishing Company
Dubuque, Iowa

C O N T E N T S

P R E F A C E

Crucial to succeeding in technical areas today is the ability to communicate effectively via the written document, be it an informal memo or a formal proposal. It is thus essential that prospective writers in technical fields be guided in the appropriate and effective use of technical rhetoric.

THE TECHNICAL WRITER'S GUIDE WITH EXERCISES is designed to provide students in technical writing courses explanations (rules), examples, and practice in problematic areas of grammar, mechanics, and usage. While handbooks, workbooks, diagnostic/achievement test packages, and exercises abound for use in "general" writing classes and even in business communication courses, materials of this kind that reflect the vocabulary used in fields of science and industry are limited.

Technical writing courses are usually considered "advanced" level courses, and students are expected to **know** the basic rules of grammar, mechanics, and usage. However, even on this level, students still make errors and present **far** more deficiencies than we would consider desirable. The exercises that are presented here will help students to recognize problem areas and will provide them the editing skills necessary to eliminate mistakes in their writing.

Although many of these problems occur in all types of writing, we have chosen the models that appear in **THE TECHNICAL WRITER'S GUIDE WITH EXERCISES** because they exhibit content, sentence structure, diction, and punctuation actually used in scientific research and in technical, industrial, and mechanical professions.

In addition to the problematic areas of mechanics, usage, and grammar, the book provides documentation styles for selected technical areas and general guidelines for manuscript preparation. Because of the technical content of all material used, we believe the writing involved in this text will be more "meaningful" to the technically oriented student.

Our text would be incomplete without mention of those who have assisted us in accomplishing this task. Thanks are thus due to our editor, Wes Burnham, and the production staff of Kendall/Hunt. The experience of putting this all together has been most rewarding.

Alma G. Bryant   Jane H. Duke

THE TECHNICAL WRITER'S GUIDE

WITH EXERCISES

PROBLEMS WITH USAGE

Word Choice
Appropriateness in word choice governs the use of specific terms in technical writing. Included below are words commonly misused. When in doubt, check your dictionary for the correct usage.

A lot

Commonly used to mean "much," "many," "a great deal." Because of its informality, you should avoid it in technical communication. Never write this term as one word (**alot**).

Allot

"to distribute, assign, or give"

Accept, Except

Accept is sometimes confused with **except**. To use the two correctly, remember that **accept** is to be used when you want to "agree to take," "consent to," or "willingly admit" something.

Example: The supervisor did not **accept** the excuse until the secretary produced a physician's statement.

Except is to be used to **exclude**.

Example: The software package contained everything **except** a thesaurus.

Adapt, Adept, Adopt

Adapt and **adopt** are <u>verbs</u>, with **adapt** meaning, "to adjust to something new," and **adopt** meaning, "to take as one's own." **Adept** is an <u>adjective</u>, meaning "skilled."

Example: The hospital will **adopt** a policy of locating **adept** LPN's who can **adapt** to hectic surroundings.

Advice, Advise

Advice is a <u>noun</u> that refers to "opinion" or "counsel." **Advise** is the <u>verb</u> that means "give opinion" or "counsel."

Examples: The supervisor's **advice** to the engineer was crucial to the completion of the project.

He did not **advise** the engineer to take short cuts in meeting the deadline.

Affect, Effect

These two words can be used as verbs or as nouns. Observe the following uses:

As verbs: **Affect** means "to display," "to imitate," "to put on," "to pretend to."

Example: To **affect** a Southern accent in the presence of Southerners is sometimes beneficial.

To **affect** ignorance of the perpetrator of the crime may cause harm to your character as a witness.

Also

Affect means "to influence," "to have an effect on."

Example: The President's decision will **affect** the election re-sults.

Severely cold weather **affects** the citrus crop.

Effect means "to bring about," "to make happen."

Example: The union intends to **effect** minor changes in the con-tract.

As nouns: **Affect** (as used by psychologists) means "emotion" or "emotional behavior."

Example: Without **affect**, the patient watched the replay of the accident.

Effect means "result," "consequence."

Example: The cold weather had no serious **effect** on the citrus crop.

Agree to/Agree with/Agree upon

We **agree to** terms.

Example: The competitor did not **agree to** the terms of the contract.

We **agree with** an opinion.

Example: If you **agree with** what the speaker is saying, support him.

We **agree upon** a plan.

Example: We must **agree upon** a plan of action before we cast our vote.

Almost/Most

Most is colloquial usage for **almost.** If you can substitute **almost** for **most** in your sentence, then the appropriate word is **almost.**

> **CHANGE** Budget revisions are due **most** every month.
>
> **TO** Budget revisions are due **almost** every month.

Amount/Number

Things in bulk or mass are referred to as **amount.**

Example: A large **amount** of calcium deposits was found in the patient's bones.

Things counted as individual items are referred to as **number.**

Example: The **number** of patients participating in the study was limited.

Allude/Elude

Allude means to "hint at" or "make an indirect reference to"; **elude** means to "evade" or "escape from."

Examples: The manager **alluded** to an impending layoff of factory workers.

The manager **eluded** questions about a layoff of factory workers.

As per/Per

Per means "through" or "by means of," or with units of measurement "for each."

Example: You will be reimbursed for <u>per diem</u> expenses.

In business jargon, **per** and **as per** are used to mean "according to. "Avoid both expressions in technical writing.

> **INCORRECT:** As per our agreement, we will reimburse your travel expenses.
>
> **CORRECT:** As we agreed, we will reimburse your travel expenses.

As regards/With regard to/In regard to/Regarding

<u>All</u> of these forms are acceptable; however, there are some idiomatic variations that are incorrect:

INCORRECT	CORRECT
with regards to in regards to	with regard to in regard to as regards regarding

As to whether/Whether

Avoid using the redundant phrase **as to whether**. Use **whether** instead.

CHANGE   As to whether the factory will recall the defective parts is unknown.

TO   **Whether** the factory will recall the defective parts is unknown.

Being as/Being that

These are nonstandard phrases which should be avoided. Use instead the words **since** or **because**.

CHANGE   Being that the proposal was four days late, the company was forced into bankruptcy.

TO   **Because** the proposal was late, the company was forced into bankruptcy.

Can not/Cannot

The preferred form is **cannot** (one word).

Comprise/Compose

Do not confuse **comprise** ("to include," "to contain," "to consist of") with **compose** ("to constitute," "to create," " to make up the whole").

CHANGE   The committee is **comprised** of 10 members.

TO   The committee is **composed** of 10 members.

Continual/Continuous

Continual means "repeated regularly and frequently."

Example: The continual diet of low-fat foods improved the health of the patient.

Continuous means "uninterrupted action."

Example: The **continuous** roaring of the machine caused the night-watchman to fall asleep.

Credible/Creditable

If something is believable, it is **credible**.

Example: The witness gave a **credible** account of the accident.

If something is worthy of praise, it is **creditable**.

Example: The quarterback was praised for his **creditable** performance.

Criterion/Criteria

A **criterion** is "a standard, rule, or test on which a judgment can be based." **Criteria** is always plural; therefore, make sure verbs, pronouns, etc., agree.

INCORRECT: The **criteria** for acceptance was determined by the panel.

CORRECT: The **criteria** for acceptance were determined by the panel.

Decided/Decisive

Decided - "clear cut," "without a doubt," "unmistakable."

Decisive - "conclusive."

Example: The **decided** superiority of the company's proposal gave the company a **decisive** advantage over all competitors.

Differ from/Differ with

Differ from indicates that two items are not identical; **differ with** indicates disagreement between persons.

Example: The concrete used in the foundation for the warehouse **differs from** that used in the main building.

Example: The loading dock manager **differed with** his supervisor on the implementation of the new schedule.

Discreet/Discrete

Discreet means "having or showing judicious reserve in speech or behavior."

Example: Executives are wise to be **discreet** in their personal contact with employees.

Discrete refers to something that is "separate" and "distinct."

Example: There is a **discrete** difference in the final draft of the proposal.

Due to/Because of

Due to means "caused by" and is an adjective phrase that should not be used in place of the prepositional phrase **because of**.

Example: The project's failure was **due to** poor administrative supervision.

Example: **Because of** excessive absences, the secretary was terminated.

Eminent/Imminent/Immanent

Eminent - "distinguished."

Example: Nobel Prize winners are **eminent** individuals.

Imminent - "near," "about to occur."

Example: Realizing his death was **imminent**, the pilot jumped because of fear.

Immanent - "inherent" or "subjective."

Example: Survival is an **immanent** characteristic of all species.

Explicit/Implicit

Explicit - refers to a meaning directly stated.

Example: Directions for installing the heat pump were **explicit** enough for a novice to understand.

Implicit - refers to a meaning conveyed but not directly expressed.

Example: The expression on the judge's face indicated his **implicit** disapproval of the matter.

Fewer/Less

Use **fewer** to refer to items that can be counted and **less** to refer to the measurement of things in "bulk" or "mass."

Example: The typist made **fewer** mistakes on the fifth revision of the report.

Example: This year's production was **less** than that of last year.

In/Into

In means "inside of," and **into** means "movement to the inside of."

Example: After climbing **into** the attic, the contractor found the faulty wire **in** the heating system.

Ingenious/Ingenuous

Ingenious means "original and imaginative in design, construction, or execution." **Ingenuous**, however, means "without sophistication" or "naive."

Consider the differences in meaning of these two sentences:

His plan was **ingenious.**

His plan was **ingenuous.**

Inside/Inside of

The preferred term is **"inside"** since the **"of"** in **"inside of"** is redundant.

CHANGE The fuse is **inside of** the box.

TO The fuse is **inside** the box.

In spite of/Despite

Both expressions mean "not withstanding" and are interchangeable. <u>Do</u> <u>not</u> use the idiomatic blend **in despite of.**

Interface

Interface as a verb means "to interact or coordinate smoothly" and is used to describe the action between devices and systems. <u>Do</u> <u>not</u> use **interface** as a synonym for <u>collaborate</u>, <u>interact</u>, or <u>cooperate</u>.

INCORRECT: The research teams will **interface** with each other on the project.

CORRECT: The research teams will **collaborate** on the project.

Irregardless/Regardless

Remember that **irregardless** is nonstandard because of its redundancy. Use **regardless** instead.

CHANGE The company must change its image **irregardless of the cost.**

TO The company must change its image **regardless....**

Its/It's

Do not confuse the personal pronoun **its** with the contraction of **it is (it's)**.

Example: **It's** mandatory that the firm change **its** image.

Loose/Lose

Loose - "unfastened" (always an <u>adjective</u>).

Example: The **loose** wiring caused the connection to be faulty.

Lose - "be deprived of," "fail to win."

Example: We don't want to **lose** the opportunity to win the government contract.

Maybe/May be

Maybe means "perhaps."

Example: **Maybe** the vice president will be appointed to chair the committee.

May be is a verb phrase and is always written as two words.

Example: The vice president **may be** appointed to chair the committee.

Medium/Media

A **medium** is an intervening substance through which something is transmitted or accomplished." **Media** is the plural of this word and must always take a plural verb (and plural pronouns).

Needless to say

This expression is often used to convey irony in speech and informal writing; however, <u>do</u> <u>not</u> clutter your technical prose with <u>needless</u> information.

Notable/Noticeable

Notable - "worthy of notice."

Example: The negotiation of the arbitrator was **notable**.

Noticeable - "readily observed."

Example: The 84-story building is **noticeable** for miles.

Observance/Observation

Observance - "performance of a duty, custom, or law."

Example: The **observance** of all legal holidays will be negotiated in the next board meeting.

Observation - "act of noticing or recording something."

Example: The lab **observation** report must be carefully proofed for correct documentation.

Orient/Orientate

Although both words have the same meaning and may be used interchangeably, use the shorter form, **orient**, in technical writing.

Parcel/Partial

A **parcel** is a package or a portion of land. **Partial** is an adjective that means "not total."

Example: The board members approved the purchase of three **parcels** of land in Texas.

Example: This is a **partial** shipment. The remainder of your order will be delivered within a week.

Personal/Personnel

Personal (<u>adjective</u>) - refers to "an individual person."

Example: **Personal** leave may not exceed three days.

Personnel (<u>noun</u>) - refers to a group of individuals employed in a company.

Example: Monthly paychecks will be available in the **personnel** office.

Principal/Principle

Principal - (1) an interest-earning amount of money.

Example: The interest rate was 16% of the **principal**.

(2) "chief," "head," "main."

Example: 1. He was appointed **principal** of the high school.

2. The **principal** concern is safety.

Principle - a "basic truth or belief," implying a standard for guiding action.

Example: Public officials must abide by the **principles** of good conduct.

Remainder/Balance

Remainder indicates that which is left after other parts have been taken away. The word **balance** may also mean **remainder** when it refers to a bank account. <u>Do</u> <u>not</u> use **balance** interchangeably with **remainder**.

INCORRECT: The **balance** of the report is forthcoming.

CORRECT: The **remainder** of the report is forthcoming.

Site/Sight/Cite

Site, a noun, is the "place of an event." **Sight**, as a noun, means "field of vision." **Cite** is a verb that means "to mention as support, illustration, or proof."

Examples: The commissioners vetoed the proposed park **site** because the land was too expensive.

The **sight** of two more eagles in the area encouraged environmentalists.

Always **cite** your sources.

Some time/Sometime/Sometimes

Some time - a "duration of time."

Example: The accident caused the officers to persist for **some time** to remove the badly tangled body.

Sometime - an "unknown, unspecified time."

Example: The packages will be delivered **sometime** next month.

Sometimes - "occasionally," "at times," "now and then."

Example: The equipment **sometimes** fails to operate properly.

Specie/Species

Specie is coined money. It is <u>not</u> the singular for **species**, which is "a fundamental category of taxonomic classification." The plural of **species** is also **species**.

INCORRECT: One **specie** of anglerfish is the goosefish.

CORRECT: One **species** of anglerfish is the goosefish.

Than/Then

Than is a conjunction used to introduce the second element of a comparison. <u>Do</u> <u>not</u> confuse it with **then,** an adverb that indicates time or consequence.

Example: The wiring took longer **than** we expected.

Example: After the wiring is complete, **then** we can install the dry wall.

There/Their/They're

There as an <u>adverb</u> specifies place.

Example: Place the instructions **there** until you are told to do otherwise.

There is also an <u>expletive</u>.

Example: **There** is the possibility that the instructions will have to be revised.

They're is the <u>contraction</u> of **they are.**

Example: Five new companies opened offices in the downtown area; **they're** hiring 1,000 employees per week.

Thus/Thusly

Both words are adverbs. Although once widely used, **thusly** is today considered an affectation and should not be used.

INCORRECT: A quorum was not reached. **Thusly,** no vote was taken.

CORRECT: A quorum was not reached. **Thus,** no vote was taken.

"Til/Till/Until

Avoid the nonstandard **'til** and the informal **till;** use **until** instead.

CHANGE Turn the screw **'til** it is secure.

TO Turn the screw **until** it is secure.

Toward/Towards

Although both words mean "in the direction of," **towards** is chiefly a British spelling.

Example: The new journal is targeted **toward** individuals in the home health care field.

Use/Utilize

Use means "to avail oneself of something." **Utilize** indicates a narrower sense: "to make useful or productive something that previously had not been."

Example: The survey crew **used** bright orange paint to mark the boundaries.

Example: This year the scientists **utilized** radio telemetry to track the range of the Florida panther.

Verbal/Oral

Verbal means "in words" and does not literally distinguish between that written and that spoken. **Oral** indicates the spoken word. Even though these words are frequently used interchangeably, in technical writing it is best to express the precise meaning.

AMBIGUOUS: We have a **verbal** contract with Marston Associates to furnish the equipment.

CORRECT: We have an **oral** contract with Marston Associates to furnish the equipment.

or

We have a **written** contract with Marston Associates to furnish the equipment.

Wait on/Wait for

Wait on is an idiom that means "to serve others." Use **wait for** to mean "to expect something or someone" or "to remain."

INCORRECT: We **waited on** the long distance conference call for two hours.

CORRECT: We **waited for** the long distance conference call for two hours.

Who's/Whose

Who's is the contraction for **who is**.

Example: **Who's** going to replace the faulty fuse?

Whose is a possessive pronoun.

Example: It is difficult to determine **whose** project should represent the company since they all are excellent.

EXERCISE 1
MASTERING WORD CHOICE

DIRECTIONS: In the following sentences underline the correct word(s) in parentheses.

1. Office policies state that we are not to (**except, accept**) collect calls.

2. How much time shall we (**alot, a lot, allot**) each speaker?

3. The firm will conditionally (**adopt, adapt, adept**) the proposal.

4. Your (**advise, advice**) regarding the problem will be appreciated.

5. The addition of new (**personal, personnel**) will (**effect, affect**) our company's production volume.

6. Do you (**agree to, agree with**) the recommendation made by the review committee?

7. Regulations are revised (**almost, most**) every day on the excavation site.

8. A large (**amount, number**) of government projects were rejected because of improper bidding.

9. (**With regard to, Regarding, In regard to**) your October 1 letter, I am responding to your request.

10. We are still undecided (**as to whether, whether**) to accept the firm's offer.

11. The foreman will (**alot, allot, a lot**) two weeks to the project.

12. The undeveloped site (**can not, cannot**) be appraised before the bids are made.

13. The firm is (**comprised, composed**) of nine departments.

14. After 12 hours of (**continual, continuous**) deliberation, the union leaders finally agreed upon a settlement.

15. Your source must be (**creditable, credible**) if the evidence you reveal is to win your case.

16. The company's (**decided, decisive**) advantage over the competition made the difference.

17. The campus cancer research hospital is a (**discreet, discrete**) unit of the university.

18. (**Due to, Because of**) widespread illness of the employees, public offices in the city were closed for two weeks.

19. Knowing that his dismissal was (**immanent, eminent, imminent**), the troubled scientist voluntarily resigned from the commission.

20. The union members reached an (**explicit, implicit**) agreement to fix prices.

21. (**Fewer, Less**) than 10 members of the staff attended the briefing.

22. Delving deeply (**in, into**) the subject, the speaker lost his audience.

23. The instructions will be just (**inside, inside of**) the front panel.

24. Certain stocks will retain their value (**irregardless, regardless**) of the market.

25. The instruction sheet should be included with (**it's, its**) proper container.

26. (**Loose, Lose**) materials should be packed securely in foam wrapping.

27. The course of action that the committee takes (**may be, maybe**) detrimental to the plans of the group.

28. The crew of engineers is making (**notable, noticeable**) progress on the construction project.

29. In (**observance, observation**) of Washington's birthday, all federal buildings will be closed today.

30. Paychecks will be available for all (**personal, personnel**) today.

31. (**Principal, Principle**) parts of the proposal were omitted.

32. Engineers are (**sometime, some time, sometimes**) required to write.

33. If (**there are, their, they're**) problems with the compressor, the cost to the customer is great.

34. (**Who's, Whose**) responsiblity is it to conduct the survey?

35. The report of the committee will not be available (**'til, till, until**) the next committee meeting.

EXERCISE 2
MASTERING WORD CHOICE

DIRECTIONS: Underline the correct word or phrase in each sentence.

1. The committee is considering the adoption of an umbrella policy that will (**affect, effect**) all division managers.

2. Welding on the St. Dominic 24-inch diameter pipeline is 75 percent complete; the (**balance, remainder**) should be finished within the next two weeks.

3. Our attorney has (**adviced, advised**) us against taking any legal action and has recommended that we (**accept, except**) the proposed settlement.

4. The right-of-way technician is currently investigating the acquisition of a 75-acre (**partial, parcel**) of land in the northwest corner of Field B-84.

5. A (**discrete, discreet**) point analysis of the program resulted in the modification of the entire network.

6. The project manager (**eluded, alluded**) to several problems his crew encountered at the construction (**sight, cite, site**).

7. According to a 1987 study, the area under investigation has experienced the extinction of three reptilian species (**due to, because of**) chemical contamination.

8. Thirty percent (**fewer, less**) building permits were issued last year (**than, then**) in the previous year. The decline was (**due to, because of**) the new tax laws.

9. The newly (**adopted, adapted**) system can be easily (**adapted, adopted**) by each department for (**its, it's**) particular needs.

10. (**With regards to, With regard to**) the recent investment option, this contract is binding.

11. The (**number, amount**) of holdings for the year were excessive.

12. (**Being that, Since**) the expenditures exceeded the budget, the president placed a freeze on all hiring.

13. The (**principle, principal**) landowner must sign the contract before action is taken.

14. (**Who's, Whose**) responsibility is it to condemn the property?

15. The committee was (**comprised, composed**) of 12 members.

16. (**Whether, As to whether**) the defects will pose a major problem will be determined by extensive road tests.

17. Final reproduction costs could not be determined, (**being that, because**) the accountant did not keep accurate records.

18. The (**continuous, continual**) breakdown of the equipment caused a delay in the completion date of the project.

19. We must not (**lose, loose**) sight of our goals.

20. How much time will you (**a lot, allot, alot**) to the project?

EXERCISE 3
MASTERING WORD CHOICE

DIRECTIONS: In the sentences below, if the underlined word or phrase is used correctly, place a **C** in the space; if incorrect, place an **X**.

_____1. To ensure that the gas meter apparatus remains in <u>continual</u> working order, we suggest a biannual maintenance schedule.

_____2. The <u>principle</u> risk posed by logging in the national forests is the reduction of wildlife habitats.

_____3. Keep me apprised of new developments in the right-of-way negotiations, <u>irregardless</u> of the time.

_____4. The timber harvest in 1984 yielded <u>less</u> pines than that harvested in 1980.

_____5. The Department of Health will conduct its <u>site</u> inspection on Tuesday, March 3.

_____6. Ms. Sievers has <u>effected</u> all of the policy changes suggested by our department.

_____7. The reason liquid radwaste cannot be easily transported <u>is because of</u> its high volatility.

_____8. Nuclei can exist only in certain <u>discreet</u> spin states, which are prescribed by the quantum theory.

_____9. Although alternative combustion techniques <u>maybe</u> available, atmospheric fluidized bed boilers eliminate the need for elaborate combustion modifications.

___10. We are <u>waiting on</u> the weather to clear before we lay the concrete foundation.

___11. The consultant from Monroe Enterprises will visit your department <u>some time</u> next week.

___12. The root of one <u>specie</u> of stillingia, a perennial shrub, has been used medicinally as an emetic and cathartic.

___13. As a basic food element, sucrose supplies approximately 13 percent of all the energy man derives from foods. <u>Thusly</u>, it is not surprising to learn that more sucrose is manufactured annually than any other organic compound.

___14. <u>Per our discussion</u>, the recent rise in production costs may force us to increase our retail prices.

____15. As per our telephone conversation, I have incorporated into the contract the changes you requested.

____16. The enclosed information sheet should help orientate you to the scope of our wetlands project.

____17. The utilization of robots to x-ray weld seams can improve your safety rating.

____18. The Maxwell Corporation's training software series is targeted toward novice computer users interested in learning the various applications of spreadsheets.

____19. If the final phase of the Scottswood Elementary School construction project is not completed according to the schedule, Hamilton Construction will be effected.

____20. Needless to say, the priority of the research team is to develop a gasket that can withstand the excessive temperatures produced by the incinerator system.

EXERCISE 4
MASTERING WORD CHOICE

DIRECTIONS: In the sentences below, if the underlined word or phrase is used correctly, place a **C** in the space; if incorrect, place an **X**.

_____1. Our legal department has advised us that although the contract between Metro Piping and Chem-Lab, Inc. was made <u>verbally</u>, it is legally binding and must be honored.

_____2. After completing the hydrostatic test, the technician submitted a written report of his <u>observances</u>.

_____3. According to some analyses, the problems associated with terminal storage of high-level radioactive waste <u>maybe</u> caused by political indecision rather than by the lack of sophisticated technology.

_____4. The use of computers as a <u>media</u> for generating architectural blueprints is becoming increasingly more common.

_____5. Because of the <u>discreet</u> specifications you require for additional storage area to your plant, we feel that our proposal offers the most practical approach.

_____6. To maintain employee efficiency and morale, supervisors should <u>interface</u> frequently with their staff members.

_____7. <u>Irregardless</u> of the expense, the flanges on pipe sector 42-C of the Clear Lake system must be replaced.

_____8. The assay of subterranean rock revealed the presence of shale <u>like</u> we expected.

_____9. Larvae of the syrphus fly, many species of which are of economic importance, live in <u>lose</u> decaying wood or in the soft stems of some plants.

_____10. Because of several <u>ingenuous</u> programming adjustments, the efficiency of the clerks in the royalties and revenue division has increased 12 percent.

_____11. Economic considerations motivated the project manager to delay acquisition of the land <u>partial</u>.

_____12. The <u>immanent</u> threat of Hurricane Connie reversing course caused the evacuation of the off-shore crews working in the Gulf of Mexico.

_____13. Ginger <u>most</u> always reduces skin irritation.

_____14. Mr. Galloway's decision to award the construction contract was based on a single <u>criteria</u>: the earliest completion date.

_____15. Although Mr. Simon was one of the company's most productive accountants, he was never promoted because of his <u>continual</u> rudeness to fellow workers.

_____16. When a number of valley glaciers flow together at the foot of a mountain range, <u>there</u> referred to as piedmont glaciers.

_____17. <u>In</u> <u>spite</u> <u>of</u> the security precautions, classified information related to the project 14-B-22 was obtained by Land Marine, one of our biggest competitors.

_____18. <u>May</u> <u>be</u> the defects in the ventilation system can be repaired.

_____19. Recommendations made by the comptroller for authorizing expenditures over $500 <u>differs</u> greatly <u>with</u> those submitted by the outside auditing firm.

_____20. The operating manual for the new gas detection device <u>comprises</u> ten chapters.

Bureaucratese

Because the major goal in technical writing is to communicate information with clarity and directness to the reader, it is important to develop a style that is compatible with that aim. All too often, writers believe that "glitzy" rhetoric enhances their style. In reality, its use displaces the focus of the problem at hand and forces the reader to sift through unnecessary verbiage to interpret the message. Writing that uses such wordiness is often associated with government and legal correspondence and reports, hence the label "bureaucratese." Below is a list of some affected phrases that should be avoided. To the right of each problem phrase is a more direct expression that can be substituted.

a majority of	most
a number of	several, some, many
arrive at a conclusion	conclude
as a means of	for
at an early date	soon
attached please find	attached is
at the conclusion of	after, following
at the present time	now
at this point in time	now
based on the fact that	because
bring to a conclusion	conclude
consensus of opinion	consensus
demonstrates a tendency to	tends to
despite the fact that	although
due to the fact that	because
during the course of	during
during the time that	during, while
effectuate improvement of	improve
exhibits a tendency	tends
for the purpose of	for
give consideration to	consider
having the capability to	can
impact on	affect
in connection with	about, concerning
in order to	to
in regard to	about, regarding
in the event that	because
in view of the fact that	because
it is often the case that	often
it is our opinion that	we think that, we believe that
it is our understanding that	we understand that
make reference to	refer to
of the opinion that	think that
prior to	before
relative to	about, regarding
so as to	to
subsequent to	after
take into consideration	consider
until such time	until

EXERCISE 1
MASTERING BUREAUCRATESE

DIRECTIONS: The following letter contains several "bureaucratic" or wordy expressions. Identify the problem phrases by underlining them. Then, correct them by writing an acceptable substitute above each error.

                              LMR, INC.
                      14561 Japonica Boulevard
                       Houston, Texas 77017
                          July 6, 1988

Lloyd H. Jenkins
Intrastate Wholesale
Post Office Box 54655
Alvin, Texas 77327

Dear Mr. Jenkins:

During the course of our recent meeting, you raised a number of questions in regard to the efficacy and efficiency of your current communication system. On your behalf, we have researched the available alternatives.

It is often the case that the upgrading of equipment does not necessarily result in a substantial improvement of quality. However, in view of the fact that great strides have been achieved in communications technology since the installation of your original system, it is our opinion that you should take into consideration the replacement of your copper wire transmission system.

Subsequent to our research, we have arrived at the conclusion that fiber optics transmission has the capability to reduce your communications expenditures as well as to impact on the effectiveness of your communication network.

23

Attached please find a summary relative to fiber optics followed by a detailed cost estimate for replacing your present copper wire system with an optical fiber system. Also make reference to the schedule in Appendix A as a means of determining a mutually acceptable start-up date.

In the event that you have questions in connection with the enclosed information, please do not hesitate to call.

Sincerely,

L. Max Reid

EXERCISE 2
MASTERING BUREAUCRATESE

DIRECTIONS: Rewrite the following memo, eliminating the tedious and awkward expressions.

MEMO

TO: L. J. Rankin, Vice President

FROM: Al Destry, Operations Supervisor

DATE: July 8, 1988

RE: PRELIMINARY BUDGET

As per your request, please find attached Operations' preliminary budget for fiscal year 1989. At this point in time, our projections for new equipment do not include telemetering stations due to the fact that Engineering has not completed its new specifications guidelines. Until such time as we receive this information, we cannot determine how it will impact on other budget items. We will send you our revisions at an early date. (It is our understanding that Engineering will deliver these guidelines by the end of next week.)

AD/wz
Attachment

2

PROBLEMS WITH STYLE

AMBIGUITY
Ambiguous writing occurs when two or more interpretations can be made from a single word or phrase. Two of the more common forms of ambiguity are **vague pronoun reference** and **mismodification**.

Pronoun Reference
A **pronoun** is the part of speech that takes the place of a **noun** (antecedent). The **antecedent** is the first noun agreeing in number, case, and gender that precedes the **pronoun**.

NOTE: A **pronoun** <u>cannot</u> take the place of a complete idea, action, or process.

Ambiguity often occurs when **demonstrative pronouns** (<u>this</u>, <u>these</u>, <u>that</u>, <u>those</u>) are used as substitutes for previously stated ideas, actions, or processes.

> **INCORRECT:** Wood tar is made by heaping the roots and wood of the beech and pine into a canonical stack depressed at the center, covering with earth, and firing. <u>This</u> is now more economically conducted by distillation.

The ambiguity in this example occurs because, gramatically, <u>this</u> refers to <u>firing</u>, the pronoun's logical antecedent. Correct errors of this kind by providing a **noun** that represents the stated idea, action, or process <u>after</u> the **pronoun**.

> **CORRECT:** <u>This process</u> is now more economically conducted by distillation.

NOTE: Proofread carefully to make certain all demonstrative pronouns are properly referenced.

MISMODIFICATION
A modifier is any word, phrase, or clause that qualifies or limits another word, phrase, or clause. Because of their restrictive function, modifiers should be located as near as possible to the word or group of words they are meant to modify.

Mismodification can cause both ambiguity and awkwardness in your writing. There are two major types of modification errors: **misplaced modifiers** and **dangling modifiers**.

Misplaced modifiers occur when they can be interpreted to modify a word or word group other than the one intended by the writer.

> **INCORRECT:** Our geologist noted the lime formations <u>surveying the proposed drilling site.</u>

The ambiguity in this sentence arises because it is the <u>geologist</u>, not the <u>lime formations</u>, who did the surveying.

Correct errors of this kind by placing the modifier in the sentence next to the element you intend it to modify.

> **CORRECT:** <u>Surveying the proposed drilling site</u>, our geologist noted the lime formations.

Dangling modifiers, unlike **misplaced modifiers**, have no logical word or phrase to modify.

> **INCORRECT:** <u>Having witnessed the explosion,</u> the foreman's statement was taken by the safety investigators.

This particular phrase is awkward because it illogically modifies <u>statement</u>. The writer obviously meant to modify <u>foreman</u>. In this sentence, however, there is no foreman--only the <u>foreman's statement</u>.

Correct **dangling modifiers** in one of two ways:

1. Provide a <u>logical</u> referent for the modifier and restructure the main clause.

> **CORRECT:** <u>Having witnessed the explosion</u>, the foreman gave his statement to the safety investigators.

2. Change the **dangling modifier** to a **dependent clause**.

> **CORRECT:** <u>After the foreman witnessed the explosion</u>, his statement was taken by the safety investigators.

EXERCISE 1
MASTERING AMBIGUITY (PRONOUN REFERENCE)

DIRECTIONS: Correct the following sentences if they are incorrect.

1. Sparrow hawks, a genus of long-legged, short-winged falcons, prey on small birds, sparrows, mice, and insects. They are abundant in Great Britain and Ireland.

2. An experimental method of exhibiting the spheroid state begins by heating a metallic disk and cautiously dropping water on it. This should be slightly concave.

3. Several company officials agreed on the next day to make honorary promotions an annual event.

4. Editors remind engineers regularly to proofread their documents.

5. The lawyer whom she called eagerly agreed with her.

6. Compensation for our services is equivalent to 5% of the total construction cost. This is competitive with other local firms that charge from 6% - 8%.

7. Atmospheric fluidized bed boilers have overcome two fundamental limitations. They can be made to control sulfur dioxide and nitrogen oxide emissions within the combustion chamber.

8. The civil engineers agreed with the electrical engineers that it was their responsibility to secure the service of a legal advisor.

9. Because the attorneys did not agree with the judges, they should be allowed to clear up the matter.

10. The carpenter told the painter that he was not happy with his work.

EXERCISE 2
MASTERING AMBIGUITY (MISMODIFICATION)

DIRECTIONS: Correct the following sentences if they are incorrect.

1. In the past ten years, Armden's Furniture has grown into an eight-store chain, each having its own warehouse.

2. Reviewing the sales record, it is apparent that each sales person has increased personal performance in the last quarter.

3. To achieve impartial results in a survey that questions the respondent's ethics, anonymity should be assured.

4. Flowering in the early spring, the dogwoods in the lower east valley were inspected for larvae infestation.

5. To manage successfully, the goals of others need to be considered.

6. Water was finally reached at 435 feet, drilling at a 45° angle.

7. To counteract the patient's allergic reaction to the dye, antihistamine was administered until the symptoms abated.

8. Keeping these progressive ideas in mind, the company's new pack-
   aging plant will not have to be updated for many years.

9. Before completing this application, please read the accompanying
   letter.

10. Before accessing the system, your personal identification number
    must be entered into the computer.

EXERCISE 3
MASTERING AMBIGUITY (MISMODIFICATION)

DIRECTIONS: Correct the following sentences if they are incorrect.

1. After extracting the oil, the remaining mealy portion of the jojoba seed represents a potential food source, containing 30% protein.

2. A phagocyte is a particular white blood cell found in the mammalian blood stream, which can engulf and destroy bacteria, poisons, and foreign matter that enters the body.

3. After pressing, the paper is fully formed and is then carried through a series of heated rolls, which complete the drying.

4. Cholesterol and its derivatives are secreted through the oil glands of the skin, lubricating and protecting the hair and skin.

5. A man-made laser system has recently been developed to provide ground-based telescopes with the same sharp images received by space-based telescopes.

6. Used primarily as a sand blast abrasive, the United States' production of staurolite is confined to Clay County, Florida.

7. Flowing from the Raton Mountains in the northeast section of New Mexico, the survey team will plot the natural boundaries formed by the Cimarron River.

8. Pressured by local citizen groups, Savannah Docks Transport has agreed to renovate its highway fleet system.

9. The safety coordinator has established guidelines for meter readers that will be effected on March 1.

10. While laying underground cable, the power supply to the building was temporarily disconnected.

EXERCISE 4
MASTERING AMBIGUITY (MISMODIFICATION)

DIRECTIONS: Correct the following sentences if they are wrong.

1. Applying the chemicals carefully, the mildew dissolved.

2. Johnston and Perry studied the thermo-mechanical reliability of plastics working under a grant from AmCom Cooperative.

3. The inspector only needs to check the electrical conduits before a certificate of occupancy is issued.

4. By exposing them to vinyl chloride, cancer was induced in laboratory rats.

5. A chart is included with the equipment, which lists parts and prices.

6. Always take proper safety precautions. While welding, eye-protective goggles must be worn.

7. The hydrostatic test was run after receiving the welder's completion report.

8. Modified according to the consultant's specifications, the crew assembled the electrical network.

9. Dawson Construction has designed an efficient and cost-effective building for your company, which we know will improve your operation.

10. The fish species were identified and specimens tagged after completing the dive.

PARALLEL STRUCTURE

Use **parallel structure** for sentence elements with the same grammatical structure. Sentences that contain **coordinating conjunctions** pose faulty parallelism problems if you are not careful to make the connecting elements parallel. The most common **coordinating conjunctions** are **and, but, or,** and **nor.**

Example: The property was appraised by <u>an appraiser</u> and <u>an engineer</u>.

The reader expects a <u>noun</u> to follow **and** because a <u>noun</u> preceded it.

Example: The property must be <u>surveyed</u> and <u>appraised</u>.

The reader expects a <u>verb</u> to follow **and** because a <u>verb</u> preceded it. The same principle applies to other sentence parts, such as **infinitives, participles, and clauses.**

INFINITIVES: <u>To be independent</u> and <u>to be successful</u> are two major goals of every first-year engineer.

PARTICIPLES: We can appreciate our college instructors <u>striving to instill knowledge</u>, <u>bending over backward to make us understand</u>, and <u>remaining calm when our love of the subject does not come up to their expectations</u>.

CLAUSES: The engineer <u>who communicates well with his associates</u> and <u>who expresses his ideas with accuracy and precision to his employers</u> is the one who will excel in his career.

A major problem occurs when you fail to make elements connected by **correlative conjunctions** parallel:

    either...or
    neither...nor
    whether...or
    both...and
    not only...but also

CHANGE Most college home economics courses are <u>either</u> revised to meet today's demands <u>or</u> being eliminated altogether.

TO Most college home economics courses are <u>either</u> being revised to meet today's demands <u>or</u> being eliminated altogether.

Be careful to make parallel a series of three or more main elements.

CHANGE She preferred to type, to take dictation, and everything involving office management.

TO She preferred to type, to take dictation, and to manage the office.

EXERCISE 1
MASTERING PARALLEL STRUCTURE

DIRECTIONS: If necessary, rewrite the sentences to achieve parallel structure.

1. The installation of a floor curb will protect the walls from transport equipment damage and for maximum air circulation.

2. Monday's staff meeting was held to explain changes in the company's vacation policy, for providing assistance to newer employees, and addressing employee complaints.

3. You should read the contract thoroughly, initial the revisions, and then put your signature on the agreement letter.

4. The digital guitar implements a microchip to create sound, nylon strings to eliminate tuning, and a transpose control to switch key.

5. Subjects were instructed in techniques to achieve relaxation, positive thinking, and meditation.

6. Occasional audio dropouts, the continual occurrence of video "glitching," and uneven editing detracted from the professionalism of the production.

7. Robotic exploration of Mars, development of a full-scale space station, and the search for extraterrestrial intelligence represent some expenditures of the space program.

8. Standard features on our new model include auxiliary lighting, latched windows, and an instrument panel that is color-coded.

9. A racing heart and knees that go weak are symptomatic in persons expericing Stendahl's Syndrome.

10. Researchers are experimenting with holographically redirected light to grow greenhouse plants and in buildings to improve lighting and to reduce energy expenditures.

11. Several ecobiologists on our staff have received a grant to tape record and make an analysis of the territorial honk of the Canadian goose.

12. That it's too bulky, that it's too heavy, and that it's too difficult to maintain stability are some excuses photographers give for not using a tripod.

13. Our nesting study examined three criteria: the size and shape of the nest box, its location in the forest, and what it was made of.

14. The positive features of the seminar included the definition of statistical terms, methods and levels of measuring were explained in detail, and various types of data sets were described.

15. Volcanic eruptions, forest and grass fires, putrefying vegetation and dust storms are natural sources of air pollution.

16. Overall, the computer graphics were so crude that they were a distraction rather than helpful.

17. Consumption of electricity worldwide has increased not only in technologically advanced societies but also because more nations have embraced industrialization.

18. Sulfur dioxide emissions can be reduced by one of the following methods: change to a fuel, such as natural gas, that has a low sulfur content; the use of coal or oil that has been desulfurized; increase its dispersion by erecting tall stacks; or flue-gas desulfurization systems.

19. The article analyzes the problems from a historic as well as a cultural perspective.

20. The report needs to be revised, to be retyped, and submission to the proper office by noon.

EXERCISE 2
MASTERING PARALLEL STRUCTURE

DIRECTIONS: Make the necessary changes to make the following sentences parallel.

1. The patient may seem withdrawn and in a depressed mood months after the surgery.

2. Two objectives of the project are to update the software and increased data output.

3. Consultants for the firm did not realize that the chief executive officer was a fraud and had lied to them to encourage them to accept the offer.

4. By "docking" 10% of each employee's pay was the manager's way of protesting the strike.

5. Each candidate for the position must be industrious, intelligent, and have poise to be an effective orator.

6. The software that is purchased must be used for word processing, a spreadsheet, and a database.

7. Winning proposals will be judged on their accuracy, their attention to details, and how much they will cost.

8. Before accepting the position, you should consider whether you can survive on such a meager salary, perform at your best, and if the move will be beneficial in the long run.

9. The new president is energetic, industrious, and the employees respect him.

10. He plans to provide excellent benefits to the employees, to give adequate incentive bonuses, and providing a role model for members of his firm.

EXERCISE 3
MASTERING PARALLEL STRUCTURE

DIRECTIONS: Make the necessary changes to make the following sentences parallel.

1. They did not consider it essential to achieve a highly precise representation in terms of the total employed population because their aim was to compose the responses of major groups rather than depicting the responses of the general population of employed persons.

2. The number of students attending two-year colleges and who hold jobs is increasing.

3. The proposed system has proven to be reliable and to have a very low maintenance cost.

4. The purpose here is to analyze the damages of insect repellants and how to use safe alternatives of repelling insects.

5. Water must be added to the hole for two reasons: to form a slurry of the cuttings and also for lubrication.

6. Several advantages of polyethlene pipe include its lack of field joints, less costly installation, and it does not corrode.

7. To maintain the protection of underground piping, several measures should be taken: tape all bare metal; insulate service lines at meter swivels; and no contact between gas lines and other lines.

8. Profits from joint ventures, the impact of higher market prices, and reduced exploration expenses account for our firm's improved financial status.

9. Our recent operational success is due to our compliance with federal, state, and local regulations; the correction of previous waste problems; and from reducing our long-range liabilities.

10. The L.E.L. portion of the meter operates on the wheat-stone bridge principle, and a platinum catalytic resistor is used.

SUBORDINATION

Sometimes it becomes necessary to subordinate one idea to another when sentences are combined. Effective subordination eliminates wordiness and shows more precisely the relationship between ideas. The **noun clause**, the **adjective clause**, and the **adverb clause** are subordinate clauses.

1. **Noun clauses** are usually introduced by words such as <u>who</u>, <u>how</u>, <u>whose</u>, <u>whom</u>, <u>which</u>, <u>that</u>, <u>whoever</u>, <u>whomever</u>, <u>what</u>, <u>whatever</u>, <u>why</u>, or <u>where</u>. These clauses function in the same capacity as a noun.

   EXAMPLES: a. <u>Whatever the cost</u>, we will pay. (direct object)

                    b. The expression on the faces of the jury often indicate <u>whether the verdict is favorable</u>. (direct object)

2. **Adjective clauses** are usually introduced by such words as <u>who</u>, <u>whom</u>, <u>that</u>, <u>which</u>, or <u>whose</u>. Such a clause follows the noun or pronoun that it modifies; otherwise, the sentence sense becomes confusing. (See **MISMODIFICATION section.**)

   CHANGE   The most lucrative jobs are posted on the bulletin board which blue collar workers seek daily.

   TO   The most lucrative jobs, which blue collar workers seek daily, are posted on the bulletin board.

3. **Adverb clauses** are usually introduced by such words as <u>since</u>, <u>when</u>, <u>if</u>, <u>because</u>, <u>although</u>, or <u>so that</u>. These clauses modify verbs, adjectives, and adverbs.

   COMMON SUBORDINATING CONJUNCTIONS

after	because	so that	when
although	before	that	whenever
as	if	though	while
as if	in order that	unless	where
as though	since	until	wherever

   These clauses can be placed at the <u>beginning,</u> in the <u>middle</u>, or at the <u>end</u> of the sentence.

EXAMPLES: a. When the company car is not available, the engineer has to use his own car. **(Beginning)**

              b. The engineer, when the company car is not available, has to use his own car. **(Middle)**

              c. The engineer has to use his own car when the company car is not available. **(End)**

NOTE the punctuation in each example.

In addition to using subordinating clauses to improve your writing style, you can also use other constructions, such as <u>appositives</u> and <u>prepositional</u> <u>phrases</u>, to produce clear, concise prose.

CHANGE   Cliff Daily is the foreman of the construction crew. He has over 22 years' experience in commercial building construction.

TO   Cliff Daily, <u>the foreman of the construction crew</u>, has over 22 years' experience in commercial construction. **(APPOSITIVE)**

OR

TO   Cliff Daily, <u>with over 22 years experience in commercial building construction</u>, is the foreman of the construction crew. **(PREPOSITIONAL PHRASE)**

EXERCISE 1
MASTERING SUBORDINATION

DIRECTIONS: Rewrite the following sentences, placing the subordinate clause in a **different** position.

1. Although the utility company promised to lower the rates, monthly charges were increased by 10%.

2. Leasing is an option that the management has not considered.

3. Employees are expendable when the employer needs to cut back on expenditures.

4. While first-year engineers are in their first six months on the job, job performance is monitored frequently.

5. Corporate employees who aspire to move up the "corporate ladder" must be willing to travel when the need arises.

EXERCISE 2
MASTERING SUBORDINATION

DIRECTIONS: Using subordination to clarify relationships among ideas and to eliminate wordiness, revise the following paragraph.

Our research team replicated the experiment "Phonetic Symbolism in Natural Languages." It was first performed in 1975. We used the Chinese, Czech, and Hindi data published in the original study. We then attempted to verify those data and relied solely on the resources available at this university. We asked a professor of both Chinese and Czech to review the data for these languages. He graciously agreed. He found the translations acceptable. One of our team members speaks Hindi as her native language. She was, therefore, a natural choice to examine the vocabulary list. She reported some unfamiliar translations. Another team member had been in the Peace Corps, where he learned Hindi. He also reviewed the word list. He recognized only half of the translations. However, he acknowledged that his Hindi had undergone attrition. These recognition problems may be explained by one of two factors. One is that of dialectical differences. The other is the possibility of a language shift over a 30-year period. This second hypothesis implies a drastic and dramatically rapid change; consequently, we did not seriously consider it. Time limitations prevented further investigation of the Hindi data.

EXERCISE 3
MASTERING SUBORDINATION

DIRECTIONS: Combine the information in each set of sentences to form a single, logical sentence.

1. We translated the pairs of Arabic antonyms.
   We used a dictionary to make the translations.
   Three native speakers of Arabic examined the data.
   The speakers concurred on the accuracy of the translations.

2. The construction cost is based on current market rates.
   Wages for labor and costs of materials are included in the total price.
   Heavy equipment rental fees are also covered.
   In addition, the cost of clean-up is included.

3. Amplifiers, modulators, and oscillators are active electronic circuits.
   The operation of these circuits demands a constant source of energy.
   The primary source of this energy is alternating current.

4. LaserColor is a relatively new reproduction process.
   Lasers are used to translate a 35-mm slide into electronic signals.
   These signals are manipulated to expose a negative.

5. The core is one component of optical fiber.
   The core exists at the exact center of the fiber.
   The function of the core is to guide the light signal.
   Another purpose of the core is to transmit the bulk of the energy.
   The diameter of the core is anywhere from 2 to 120 micrometers.

6. There are few native speakers of Gaelic left in the world.
    Gaelic remains an interesting language because of its word struc-
    tures.
    Gaelic words have unusually long consonant and vowel clusters.

7. Alcohol is a central nervous system depressant.
    Alcohol is the most widely abused drug in our society.
    Some effects of alcohol are liver malfunctions, gastritis, and
    apnea.
    Apnea is the suspension of respiration.

8. A cumulonimbus is an extremely dense cloud.
    This type of cloud forms vertically.
    The top of the cloud is glaciated.
    The cumulonimbus produces heavy rains, lightning storms, and hail
    storms.

9. Niello is a black alloy.
    The base of the alloy is sulfur.
    The sulfur may be mixed with copper, silver, or lead.
    Niello is used as an ornamental inlay for metal surfaces.

10. The thermite weld requires no outside heat source.
    This type of weld allows a copper conductor to be welded to
    steel, cast iron, or another copper conductor.
    Because it requires no outside heat source, the thermite weld is
    ideal for use in the field.

3

PROBLEMS WITH AGREEMENT

Problems with agreement may occur between several grammatical relationships. The most common agreement errors appear between pronouns and their antecedents and between subjects and verbs.

PRONOUN AGREEMENT

   1. A **pronoun** must agree with its antecedent in person, number, and gender.

   > **EXAMPLES:** A well-written <u>proposal</u> is the <u>one</u> most likely to get funded. (**Singular**)
   >
   > Well-written <u>proposals</u> are the <u>ones</u> most likely to get funded. (**Plural**)

Perhaps the most widespread pronoun agreement error is the use of plural pronouns <u>(they</u>, <u>them</u>, <u>their</u>) for singular antecedents.

   > **INCORRECT:** <u>Anyone</u> who preregisters for the seminar will receive <u>their</u> materials at no charge.
   >
   > **CORRECT:** <u>Anyone</u> who preregisters for the seminar will receive <u>his</u> materials at no charge.

Although the masculine form of the pronoun is grammatically proper, its use is often perceived as sexist. One solution to this problem is to use both feminine and masculine forms:

   > **EXAMPLE:** <u>Anyone</u> who preregisters for the seminar will receive his/her materials at no charge.

This method, however, can become cumbersome for the writer and boring for the reader. A better strategy is to make the antecedent plural.

   > **EXAMPLE:** Seminar <u>preregistrants</u> will receive <u>their</u> materials at no charge.

   2. A **pronoun** that refers to a collective noun will be **singular** or **plural**, depending on whether the referenced collective noun is meant as singular or plural. Some common collective nouns are <u>board</u>, <u>crew</u>, <u>group</u>, <u>team</u>, and <u>union</u>.

   > **CORRECT:** The board cast <u>its</u> vote to break the contract. (**As a singular group**)
   >
   > **CORRECT:** The board cast <u>their</u> votes to break the contract. (**As individuals MEANING: The board members**)

NOTE: Because both precision and clarity are major goals of technical writing, adding the word <u>members</u> after the collective noun to indicate plurality will remove any ambiguity.

3. A **pronoun** is usually plural when it refers to two or more antecedents connected by <u>and</u>.

    EXAMPLE: The administrator and the secretary took <u>their</u> vacations at separate times. **(Plural because the reference is to two individuals)**

    EXCEPTION: As an officer and a stockholder, she objected to the sale of the holdings. **(An <u>officer</u> and a <u>stockholder</u> refer to the same <u>individual</u>.)**

4. A **pronoun** that refers to two antecedents connected by <u>or</u> or <u>nor</u> will be **singular** if both antecedents are singular and **plural** if both antecedents are plural. If one antecedent is singular and the other is plural, the pronoun must agree with the antecedent closest to the verb.

    EXAMPLES: Either the foreman or the contractor will have <u>his</u> credentials with him. **(Singular)**

    Neither the contractor nor the foremen seem interested in <u>their</u> jobs. **(Plural)**

SUBJECT-VERB AGREEMENT

Remember that a singular subject takes a singular verb, and a plural subject takes a plural verb. The following are problem areas you should learn to master.

1. The **subject** and **verb** must agree even though <u>intervening words</u> separate the subject and the verb.

    CHANGE The chairman, not the members of the board, **were** responsible for the company's failure.

    TO The chairman, not the members of the board, **was** responsible for the company's failure.

2. If a **singular** subject is followed by a phrase beginning with the words <u>with</u>, <u>in addition to</u>, <u>together with</u>, or <u>as well as</u>, the verb must also be **singular**.

    EXAMPLE: The board of trustees, as well as the executive committee, **has** a stake in the hospital's success.

3. A subject that is **plural** in form but **singular** in meaning takes a **singular** verb.

    EXAMPLES: <u>One-hundred dollars</u> **is** not a bonus incentive.

    <u>Ivory Snow Flakes</u> **is** a competitor of Whisk.

    <u>Corporate news</u> **is** not always depressing.

4. If a **singular** subject is followed by a <u>plural</u> <u>complement</u>, the verb must also be **singular**.

    EXAMPLE: The frequent flyer bonus **was** three trips to Hawaii.

5. If a collective noun is used as a subject, the verb can be either **singular** or **plural**, depending on the meaning you want to convey.

    EXAMPLES: The staff **has** rejected the latest version of the contract. **(Acting as an individual body)**

                         The staff **have** submitted their resignations to the corporate body. **(Acting as individuals)**

Because both precision and clarity are major goals of technical writing, adding the word <u>members</u> after the collective noun to indicate plurality will remove any ambiguity.

Several collective nouns that particularly cause problems for some writers in determining singularity or plurality are <u>majority</u>, <u>minority</u>, and <u>number</u>. Some indefinite pronouns that may be either singular or plural, depending on their context in the sentence, are <u>all</u>, <u>any</u>, <u>most</u>, <u>neither</u>, <u>none</u>, and <u>some</u>.

If you are in doubt about the plurality of any of these words, you can consult a good dictionary, such as <u>American Heritage</u> or <u>Webster's</u>, for its particular usage rule.

6. Indefinite singular pronouns take singular verbs. <u>Each</u>, <u>every</u>, <u>everyone</u>, <u>anyone</u>, and <u>anybody</u> are some singular indefinite pronouns.

    INCORRECT: <u>Everyone</u> of the members **have vetoed** the expansion project.

    CORRECT: <u>Everyone</u> of the members **has vetoed** the expansion project.

7. Titles of works or words referred to as words require **singular** verbs.

    EXAMPLES: <u>Face the Nation</u> **is** a regular Sunday presentation on national television.

                         The term fringe benefits **does** not **apply** to your contract.

8. If two or more subjects are joined by <u>or</u> or <u>nor</u>, the verb must agree with the subject that is nearer.

    EXAMPLE: Neither the utility company nor its customers **were** pleased with the rate increase.

or

Example: Neither the customers nor the utility company **was**
pleased with the rate increase.

EXERCISE 1
MASTERING AGREEMENT

DIRECTIONS: The following sentences may contain errors in pronoun agreement, subject-verb agreement, or both. Correcting any agreement errors, rewrite the following sentences.

1. The Max Corporation will have their board meeting on April 28, in Chicago.

2. Because onomatopoetic words were not used in the experiment, this cannot account for the high frequency of correct responses.

3. Manatees are aquatic mammals. It is found in the warm coastal waters of the Atlantic Ocean and the Gulf of Mexico.

4. Neither the subjects in the experimental group nor those in the control group has experienced a rise in their blood pressures.

5. Although heat was once explained by the caloric theory, thermodynamics are now defined according to atomic theory.

6. Each project engineer has the responsibility to submit their progress reports before 5 p.m. on Thursdays.

7. Subclasses of particular matter includes fine dust, coarse dust, fumes, and mists.

8. Blackstone Industries require that all of their new employees submit to drug tests.

9. Neither hydrocephaly nor microcephaly is considered to be a disease; however, they both can cause severe mental retardation.

10. After the purification process, two ounces of liquid remains in the beaker.

EXERCISE 2
MASTERING AGREEMENT

DIRECTIONS: The following sentences may contain errors in pronoun agreement, subject-verb agreement, or both. Correcting any errors, rewrite the following sentences.

1. The rapid increase in population, along with technological advancements in agriculture, have reduced the number of jobs available in rural America.

2. Johnson's ingenuity plus his integrity has won him the annual Employee of the Year Award.

3. Engineering politics provide the basis for her investigation.

4. Neither of the partners agree with the last draft of the proposal.

5. The majority of the respondents to the poll is opposed to any new legislation.

6. According to the project status report, 35% of the welds made on the Bayou Theriot 10-inch pipeline has passed inspection.

7. Langston's architectural group is known for their innovative designs.

8. Either Evans or Halsey prepared their department's budget.

9. The public has a responsibility to cast their votes on election day.

10. Dr. James Jimineg is one of the community service physicians who attend to the cardiac patients.

EXERCISE 3
MASTERING AGREEMENT

DIRECTIONS: The following sentences may contain problems in either pronoun agreement or subject-verb agreement. Rewrite the sentences to correct any agreement errors.

1. Before the creation of transmission networks, industry usually ran their own pipelines to the gas wells.

2. The denser rocks or material generally create a greater gravitational pull than the more porous areas.

3. The key to abbreviations in the Business Education Index does not include journals or periodicals. This is found in the back of the book under two separate headings.

4. Low-cost copper as well as silica flux are currently being mined and sold to a local smelter.

5. The formulation of many principles represent an attempt at the codification of generally held beliefs.

6. How do each of the results compare with the theoretical value calculated from the formula of the compound?

7. Natural gas, both compressed and liquid, are being used increasingly as a smog-free vehicular fuel.

8. Loading of the software and its installation onto the hard disk is simple.

9. The firm's commitment to environmental protection has earned them public praise.

10. Pipeline natural gas is fed through one or more city-gate stations, which meters the gas and reduces the pressure.

EXERCISE 4
MASTERING AGREEMENT

DIRECTIONS: The following sentences may contain problems in either pronoun agreement or subject-verb agreement. Rewrite the sentences to correct any agreement errors.

1. The series of articles by B. W. Booth on industry safety standards are required reading for all personnel.

2. A portion of the instructions were ambiguous.

3. The molecular theory of gases state that all gases are comprised of molecules that are widely separated relative to their sizes.

4. Gascapes are frequently used in locating gas leaks because it will detect the smallest of leaks.

5. Copper mining is one of those industries whose economic gains are at the mercy of the volatile commodities market.

6. From the experiments performed by Walsk comes the basic approach to all other investigations of this type.

7. A number of properties, polarity being one, is associated with covalent bonds.

8. Due to a power outage, some of our data was lost.

9. None of our crusher technicians has experienced a lost-time injury.

10. Systematic analysis and description of the problem is this department's responsibility.

EXERCISE 5
MASTERING AGREEMENT

DIRECTIONS: Underline the correct choice in parentheses.

1. The architect and the contractor of the multi-story building work together to assure (**its, it's**) safety.

2. The architect determines the most efficient design (**he, they**) will use.

3. The models in a technical writing text are very beneficial; (**it, they**) (**is, are**) excellent sources of reference for the technical writer.

4. Production reports must be frequently evaluated because (**it, they**) (**reveals, reveal**) much useful information to the supervisors.

5. The Central Life Insurance Company recently conducted a study to determine the amount of money (**it, they**) (**spends, spend**) on type-written documents.

6. The 27-member surface crew at the Eagle Creek Mine (**has broken, have broken**) (**its, their**) own productivity record.

7. The section on the most efficient uses of the machinery should be placed where the reader will immediately notice (**it, them**).

8. Every secretary must do the job (**they are, he/she is**) trained for.

9. The content of the report did not represent the work of (**their, its, it's**) author.

10. The formal proposal should represent (**their, its, it's**) author as a professional in the field.

4

PROBLEMS WITH PUNCTUATION

The success of any document depends on the effectiveness of its ability to convey to the reader the exact sense the writer intends. Punctuation rules are our guides to communication. The rules listed here represent some of the common problems encountered in drafting a document. If in doubt after reviewing these isolated examples, you should refer to a more complete handbook, such as the <u>St. Martin's Handbook of Technical Writing</u>.

THE APOSTROPHE `'`

The apostrophe has three distinct functions.

1. Used to form contractions, the apostrophe substitutes for the omitted letters or numbers.

they are	they're
I am	I'm
there is	there's
1960s	'60s

   Some contractions may have the same form but may have more than one meaning.

   he'd   ⌈ he had ⌉
                      ⌊ he would ⌋

   it's   ⌈ it is ⌉
                      ⌊ it has ⌋

   NOTE: In general, avoid using contractions in technical writing.

2. The apostrophe can also indicate possession. Its placement is often a source of confusion. You can apply a simple test to determine proper placement. If the noun that is to indicate possession already ends in an **s**, simply add an apostrophe.

EXAMPLE: The signature of Mr. <u>Jones</u>

Mr. <u>Jones'</u> signature

The compensation of the <u>workers</u>

<u>Workers'</u> compensation

If the noun that is to indicate possession does not end in an <u>s</u>, add an apostrophe, then the <u>s</u>.

EXAMPLE: The net profits for this year

This <u>year's</u> net profits

NOTICE that the placement of the apostrophe is <u>**not**</u> in any way determined by the singularity or plurality of the possessive noun.

To indicate possession of compound elements, the final noun receives the apostrophe or apostrophe and <u>s</u>.

EXAMPLE: <u>Carter and Dell's</u> article on compression is informative.

If, however, the compound elements need to show individual possession, mark each noun with an apostrophe or an apostrophe and <u>s</u>.

EXAMPLE: <u>Carter's</u> and <u>Dell's</u> articles on compression are informative.

Possessive pronouns <u>never</u> use apostrophes.

CORRECT FORMS: <u>ours</u>, <u>yours</u>, <u>his</u>, <u>hers</u>, <u>theirs</u>, and <u>its</u>.

NOTE: <u>It's</u> is the contraction for "it is."

3. Some plurals are formed by adding an apostrophe and an <u>s</u> to the end of the word. This use should be restricted for italicized (or underlined) words or for numbers and letters when not to do so may result in confusion.

EXAMPLES: There were too many <u>if's</u> in his proposal.

The five <u>w's</u> of journalism stand for <u>who</u>, <u>what</u>, <u>when</u>, <u>where</u>, and <u>why</u>.

THE BRACKETS $\boxed{[\,]}$

Brackets are used primarily for two purposes: (1) to set off editorial comments, additions, or substitutions included in quoted material and (2) to enclose the information within a passage already enclosed in parentheses.

EXAMPLE 1: "The apparant [sic] reason for the decline in production activity was not disclosed." **(The word Sic is used to show that the misspelling of the word apparent appeared in the original document.)**

EXAMPLE 2: In his best seller (<u>Technical Writing</u> [Scott, Foresman and Company]) Lannon includes the latest information on current style checkers.

THE COLON | : |

The colon is used to emphasize the information that follows it or to clarify the information that precedes it.

1. Use a colon at the end of an independent clause to introduce a list or series. **DO NOT** use a colon to introduce elements <u>within</u> a clause (e.g., predicate nominatives, direct objects, objects of prepositions, etc.).

    INCORRECT: Four categories of piping in a gas distribution system are: trunk mains, feeder mains, distribution mains, and service laterals.

    CORRECT: Four categories of piping in a gas distribution system are trunk mains, feeder mains, distribution mains, and service laterals.

There is one exception to this rule. If you are presenting a stacked list following the colon, you may interrupt the sentence.

    CORRECT: Four categories of piping in a gas distribution system are:

            trunk mains
            feeder mains
            distribution mains
            service laterals

2. Use a colon to separate two independent clauses when the second explains or amplifies the first.

    EXAMPLE: The training video implements an effective format: each module begins with a lecture and concludes with a dramatization.

3. Use a colon to introduce an appositive that concludes a sentence.

> **EXAMPLE:** To avoid penalties, we must meet the contract
> deadline: May 24.

THE COMMA $\boxed{,}$

The comma is an internal punctuation mark that performs a variety of
functions. Used properly, commas help the reader decode the writer's
message accurately and quickly. Yet proper comma usage--when to use
it and where to put it--often baffles many writers. Occasionally its
placement is a stylistic matter, but the following rules can help you
determine conventional usage.

1. Use a comma and a **coordinating conjunction** (and, but, or, nor,
   for, so, yet) to separate the independent clauses of a compound sentence.

   > **EXAMPLE:** Testing of regulator station equipment is required
   > annually, and complete records must be documented
   > on Form GD5-301.

   The omission of the comma will result in an error called a
   fused sentence. The omission of the conjunction will result
   in a **comma splice.**

2. Use a comma to separate items (words, phrases, or clauses) in
   a series.

   > **EXAMPLE:** Gasoline refineries, chemical plants, and carbon
   > black producers are heavy users of natural gas.

   **NOTE: Although some handbooks recommend the omission of the
   final comma before the coordinating conjunction, its retention
   is preferable in technical writing to ensure clarity.**

3. Use a comma to separate coordinate adjectives that precede a
   noun.

   > **EXAMPLE:** Formed by incomplete combustion, carbon monoxide
   > is a colorless, odorless, extremely poisonous gas.

4. Use a comma after an introductory expression (word, phrase, or
   clause) that does not flow smoothly into the main clause.

   > **EXAMPLE:** The statistical analysis completed, the research-
   > ers began to formulate their recommendations.

   **NOTICE that the omission of the comma in the above example
   will impede the clarity of the sentence.**

5. Use commas around nonrestrictive (nonessential) elements
   (words, phrases, or clauses) in a sentence.

   > **EXAMPLE:** Mr. Young, a civil engineer with over 25 years of
   > experience, has been named Vice President.

Never place commas around <u>restrictive</u> (essential) elements.

> **INCORRECT:**   The blueprints, that arrived this morning, were
> drafted by Ms. Foley.

6. Use a comma to indicate missing words in an eliptical sentence.

> **EXAMPLE:**   Last year our net profit was $540,000; this year,
> $650,000.

7. Use a comma to separate certain arrangements of elements in dates, geographic place names, and addresses.

Study the examples below for accepted placement.

<u>DATES</u>
   day, month date, year,....
The inspection was authorized on Wednesday, July 6, 1988, and completed on Wednesday, July 13, 1988.

   day, date month year....
The inspection was authorized on Wednesday, 6 July 1988 and completed on Wednesday, 13 July 1988.

   month year....
The inspection was authorized in July 1988.

<u>**GEOGRAPHIC PLACE NAMES**</u>
   city, state,....
The convention will be held in New Orleans, Louisiana, on January 12.

<u>**ADDRESSES**</u>
   city, state, zip....
Send a copy of the report to Pat Jones, P. O. Box 24831, Tampa, Florida 33617.

THE DASH ☐ -- ☐

1. Use the dash to set off a parenthetical element for emphasis, particularly if you feel commas or parentheses would be too mild.

> **EXAMPLES:**   Word processing programs--and there are
> numerous--have revolutionized the typing process.
> **(emphasis)**
>
> These three features--content, focus, and style--
> are essential for a technical document.

2. Use the dash to set off an introductory list.

> **EXAMPLE:** Content, focus, and style--these are essential
> features of a technical document.

3. Use the dash to indicate a break in thought.

> **EXAMPLE:** I recommend--in fact, I strongly recommend--
> that you document your report accurately.

THE HYPHEN | - |

1. If a word has to be divided at the right-hand margin, use a
hyphen. Divide the word only at the end of a syllable. (If
you are not sure, check your dictionary for the syllabication
of the word.)

2. Use a hyphen to join compound modifiers (adjectives) preceding
a noun.

> **EXAMPLE:** The **well-documented** proposal received national
> recognition.

> **NOTE:** If the adjective follows the noun, **do not hyphenate.**

> **EXAMPLE:** The proposal that was **well documented** received
> national recognition.

3. Use a hyphen with all words that begin with <u>self</u> or <u>quasi</u>.

> **EXAMPLES:** self-taught
> self-respect
> quasi-public

4. Use a hyphen to join an adverb-participle compound preceding a
noun.

> **EXAMPLE:** the smooth-gliding engine

> **NOTE:** If the compound modifiers are adverbs or if one of
> the words ends in <u>ly</u>, **do not hyphenate.**

> **EXAMPLES:** a very well documented report
> the superbly documented report

5. Use a hyphen to join words that begin with **ex-**, only if **ex**
means "past."

> **EXAMPLE:** ex-president

6. Use a hyphen with all fractions written as words and used as
adjectives preceding a noun.

> **EXAMPLE:** a two-thirds majority

7. Use a hyphen with ratios used as adjectives preceding a noun.

   EXAMPLE: A five-to-one vote swayed the decision.

   NOTE: If the ratio follows the noun, **do not hyphenate.**

   EXAMPLE: The decision was swayed by a vote of five to one.

8. Use a hyphen with compound numbers from twenty-one through ninety-nine.

   EXAMPLE: Thirty-five employees were fired.

9. Use the hyphen to substitute for the word <u>to</u> in expressions as these:

   Tampa-St. Petersburg express

   pp. 50-56

   1970-1979

   2:00-3:00 a.m.

10. Use a hyphen with improvised words such as these:

    made-to-order merchandise

    off-the-wall expressions

11. If a noun phrase that is used as a modifier is confusing, hyphenate to make clear your meaning.

    EXAMPLE: a personal loan service (NOT CLEAR)

    CHANGE TO: 1. a personal-loan service
    2. a personal loan-service

You have to make sure your reader interprets the meaning as either #1 or #2. There is a difference in the two, so be careful to make the right choice.

12. When noun expressions show combined responsibility, use a hyphen.

    EXAMPLES: producer-director

    secretary-treasurer

13. Use a hyphen with compound expressions indicating family relationship.

    EXAMPLES: brother-in-law

    great-grandmother

NOTE: Do not hyphenate the following:

   stepdaughter   foster father   half sister

14. Use a hyphen with numbers joined with other words to form adjectives.

   EXAMPLES: the 560-page manuscript

   the 10-year-old structure

15. Use a hyphen to express decades as words.

   EXAMPLE: The seventeen-twenties

16. Use a hyphen to prevent ambiguity with words such as the following:

   re-cover (cover again)
   recover (regain)

   re-creation (making again)
   recreation (play, leisure activity)

   re-treat (redo)
   retreat (outing)

   re-lease (lease again)
   release (let go)

17. Use a hyphen when a capital letter follows the prefix.

   EXAMPLE: mid-Atlantic

18. Use a hyphen when the prefix is a single letter, like T-Test.

THE PARENTHESES | ( ) |

Parentheses are used to enclose information that may amplify, qualify, or digress from the subject. Parenthetical information may be introduced within a sentence, or it may appear as a complete sentence.

   EXAMPLES: A standard cubic foot of gas is measured at a pressure of $\frac{1}{4}$ pound (4 oz.) above atmospheric pressure and at a temperature of 60 degrees F.

   A manometer measures pressures greater than atmospheric pressure, pressures less than atmospheric pressure, and differential pressures. (The device will not, however, measure temperatures.)

Notice the placement of periods in the last example. In this case,

76

the parenthetical information constitutes a complete sentence and is punctuated accordingly.

Parentheses are frequently used to enclose abbreviations or acronyms.

> **EXAMPLE:** Before a purchase order can be issued, an authorization for expenditure (AFE) must be approved.

THE PERIOD ⎡ . ⎤

Periods are primarily used to end declarative and imperative sentences.

> **DECLARATIVE:** Your financial statement is due on March 15.

> **IMPERATIVE:** Submit your financial statement by March 15.

Periods are also used to indicate abbreviations and initialisms written in lower case.

> **ABBREVIATIONS:** Walker Ave.

> **INITIALISMS:** a.f.e. (authorization for expenditure)
> c.e.o. (chief executive officer)

Generally, if the initialism is written in upper case (AFE or CEO), do not use periods. An exception, however, is made for geographic place names (U.S., United States) and for academic degrees (B.S., Bachelor of Science).

Do not use periods with acronyms (scuba).

Two frequent errors caused by improper period placement are the fragment and the run-on.

A **fragment** is created when a period is placed after a group of words that does not constitute an independent clause.

> **FRAGMENT:** Baker Construction's proposal was rejected. Because it did not provide a time schedule.

> **CORRECT:** Baker Construction's proposal was rejected because it did not provide a time schedule.

Advertising uses the fragment intentionally for economy as well as effectiveness. However, it is wise to avoid intentional fragments in most technical writing.

A **run-on** occurs when a writer fails to place a period between two complete sentences, one grammatical sentence "running into" the next.

RUN-ON: Mr. Mackey's performance evaluation was unfavorable he had excessive absences in the last year.

CORRECT: Mr. Mackey's performance evaluation was unfavorable. He had excessive absences in the last year.

NOTE: When a sentence ends with an abbreviation, use only <u>one</u> period at the end of the sentence.

EXAMPLE: Send the package to his address on Bergen Ave.

THE QUESTION MARK ?

The question mark is most used to end a sentence that asks a direct question.

EXAMPLE: Have you ever been convicted of a felony?

The question mark may also be used in interrogative sentences to separate certain items in a series.

EXAMPLE: What is your age? place of birth? marital status?

One of the most frequent errors in question mark usage occurs when an indirect question is punctuated as a direct question.

INCORRECT: The application asks a prospective employee if he/she has ever been convicted of a felony?

Correct this error **by using a period** instead of a question mark.

THE QUOTATION MARKS " "

1. Use quotation marks to enclose a direct quotation.

    EXAMPLE: The treasurer simply said, "I am sorry for the gross mistake I made."

2. Use quotation marks to enclose material taken exactly from the original.

    EXAMPLE: The minutes stated that "<u>all</u> employees will be held accountable."

3. Use quotation marks to enclose titles of articles and titles of chapters.

    EXAMPLES: The article "How to protect your PC equipment from a sudden power strike" appears in the March 1988 <u>Inmac</u>.

Chapter 10, "Improving Your Style," is designed to capture the attention of the writer.

4. Use quotation marks to enclose technical names on first use
<u>only</u>.

    EXAMPLE: A "forgiveness policy" was instituted to pro-
vide an option. The forgiveness policy per-
mits....

5. Use quotation marks to enclose words used as words.

    EXAMPLE: By "forgiveness" we mean....

SINGLE QUOTATION MARKS `' '`

Use single quotation marks to enclose a quotation within a quotation.

    EXAMPLE: President Reagan instructed the Cabinet, "Answer 'No'
when questioned about the proceedings."

QUOTATION MARKS WITH OTHER MARKS OF PUNCTUATION

1. Place **commas** and **periods** <u>inside</u> the quotation marks. **(THIS
RULE HAS NO EXCEPTIONS!)**

    EXAMPLES: "ENTER AT YOUR OWN RISK," read the sign on the
door of the condemned building.

                The sign on the door of the condemned building
read, "ENTER AT YOUR OWN RISK."

2. Place a semicolon or a colon outside the quotation marks.

    EXAMPLES: If possible, in technical writing avoid the use
of slang such as "corny"; use a more appropriate
word instead.

                The following statement comes from "Chapter 3":
"Proofread each chapter before saving the mate-
rial on the disk."

**If they belong to the quotation, place other marks of
punctuation <u>inside</u> the quotation marks; if they belong to the
whole sentence, place them <u>outside</u> the quotation marks.**

    EXAMPLES: "Secrets!" is the label placed on the company's
confidential files.

                "Do you plead 'innocent' or 'guilty' to the
charges?" asked the reporter.

Why did you say, "Place the printer on the right side of the monitor"?

NOTE: When a question is quoted within a question, use only <u>one</u> question mark at the end of the sentence.

THE SEMICOLON | ; |

The semicolon is often used incorrectly for a comma. Such misuse creates another, more serious problem: a fragment. Basically, the semicolon has only two functions.

1. To form a compound sentence, place a semicolon between the independent clauses.

   EXAMPLE: H. S. Sullivan postulated three prime means for attaining and maintaining security; these defenses of personality include dissociation, parataxic distortion, and sublimation.

   Another method of creating a compound sentence is the use of a comma and a coordinating conjunction placed between the independent clauses. (See **COMMA section.**) However, if either one of the independent clauses contains a comma, a semicolon before the coordinating conjunction is preferable to the comma.

   EXAMPLE: Distribution mains may be constructed of steel, plastic, or cast iron; but the latter is little used today because of its lack of flexibility, its requirement of a special joint, and its low pressure rating.

2. To separate items in a series when at least one item already contains a comma, a semicolon is used to avoid confusing the elements.

   EXAMPLE: Budget requests have been received from our offices in Baytown, TX; Lafayette, LA; and Gulfport, MS.

THE SLASH | / |

1. The slash can be used to separate parts of addresses within a sentence.

   EXAMPLE: The letter was addressed to Mr. Tim Branch/1216 North Avenue/Dayton, Ohio.

80

2. The slash can be used to show alternative items.

    EXAMPLE: The business number is 762-4319/4310.

3. The slash is often used to indicate words that have been omitted.

    EXAMPLES: miles/hour   (miler per hour)

                    c/o   (in care of)

4. The slash can be used to separate parts of dates:

    EXAMPLES: 9/29/38   (MONTH/DAY/YEAR)

EXERCISE 1
MASTERING PUNCTUATION
(BRACKETS/DASH/HYPHEN/SLASH/QUOTATION MARKS)

DIRECTIONS: Insert the correct punctuation marks where needed in the following sentences. In instances when a **dash** is needed, indicate the dash by inserting two marks (--).

1. One other thing is necessary for maintaining harmony within the workplace cleanliness.

2. Each employee must report his her absence in each monthly report.

3. These reports must be fully documented, providing date and reason it absence occurred.

4. The report stated, Eighty percent of the population will vote in the Presidential election.

5. Cigarette smoking may be harmful to your health, states the Surgeon General.

6. The instructions read, Turn the handle two notches to the right.

7. The sign reads, No U-Turn.

8. The two page letter failed to convince the creditor.

9. The ex president was a self made administrator.

10. Very few administrators today are self made.

11. What do you mean when you say document fully, asked the secretary.

12. Our former address 1921 Kennedy Avenue was destroyed by fire several weeks ago.

13. In Sherman and Johnson's <u>Modern Technical Writing</u>, Chapter 17 is entitled Letters concerning Employment and Résumés.

14. In her article, Trade Secrets, Ms. Duke reveals various techniques for increasing your working capital.

15. Each accountant is urged to keep up to date reports.

16. In the drafting department men outnumber women 3 1.

17. You may contact the publisher at this number: 837-2807 2808.

18. Officials of the new company will probably vote 5 2 to liquidate the stocks.

19. Address it to John G. Carroll 907 North Boulevard Bloomington, Indiana.

20. The instructions read, Do not waist sic time on items you do not know.

EXERCISE 2
MASTERING PUNCTUATION
DIRECTIONS: For each item write a sentence to illustrate the item requested.

1. an interruption of a thought in the middle of a sentence

2. a direct quotation

3. a quotation within a quotation

4. a quotation with an explanation inserted

5. information within a passage already enclosed in parentheses

EXERCISE 3
MASTERING PUNCTUATION
BRACKETS/HYPHEN/QUOTATION MARKS

DIRECTIONS: Insert the correct punctuation marks where needed in the following sentences.

1. The ex governor was interviewed on Face the Nation.

2. The College of Business at the local university is well endowed.

3. The well endowed College of Business at the local university attracts many evening students in its MBA program.

4. The sign over the secretarial pool read Haste makes waist sic.

5. Are periods used in the abbreviation P O Box asked the rather slow secretary.

6. More and more sub compacts infiltrated the automobile market.

7. Records show that most of our products 95 percent are selling quite well in the Northeast.

8. It took the scientist five years to research his latest article, The Major Causes of Viral Infections.

9. What an incredible discovery! exclaimed the physician.

10. Do you believe in the adage A penny saved, a penny earned asked the banker.

11. We will present a review of <u>Kennedy's Last Days</u> have you read it at our next meeting.

12. After entering the filthy room, the janitor shouted I resign!

13. Try the new IBM PS/20 your area representative will arrange a demonstration and you will fall in love with it immediately.

14. The package was addressed to the judge, stated Brian Jamison, Esq.

15. Many companies provide on-site recreation centers for their employees in order to avoid the All work and no play syndrome.

16. The drive in banking concept has enhanced our lives tremendously.

17. CAUTION! CIGARETTE SMOKING MAY BE DANGEROUS TO YOUR HEALTH did not make the impact intended.

18. For further study, read Chapter 5, Fear of Computers, before the next session.

19. Our foolproof method of concealment enhanced the product tremendously.

20. Avoid unnecessary explanations in your final copy of the report.

EXERCISE 4
MASTERING PUNCTUATION
(APOSTROPHE/COLON/COMMA/PARENTHESES/PERIOD/QUESTION MARK/SEMICOLON)

DIRECTIONS: Correcting all errors in punctuation, rewrite the following report.

HANDICAP SERVICES
FINAL PLACEMENT REPORT
FILE #415/NR

TO: David Thompson, Funding Director
FROM: Eileen March, Project Manager
DATE: 16, March 1988

SERVICE: Canine Assistance   TYPE: Hearing-ear/Retriever
ANIMAL NAME: Keeper   ID#: 649-415/NR
PROJECT PERIOD: June, 1987 - April 1988

In June, 1987 we acquired Keeper. A 2-month old approx. male Labrador retriever-Siberian husky crossbreed from the West Tanawanda, New York, SPCA, shelter. We transported the animal to Kingdom Kennels in Dade City - Florida, for assessment by trainer Nancy Rix. After conducting a preliminary evaluation of Keeper, Ms. Rix judged the animals potential to perform handicap services to be well-above average, and agreed to sponsor Keepers training.

To facilitate Keepers social adjustment during training: Ms. Rix placed the puppy in a "foster home" with Ms. Lisa Brown a handler (as well as a social worker) and Ms. Browns mature Springer Spaniel.

Keepers Florida Training Program that provided the foundation for specialized training included:

1. One on one behavior training by Ms. Rix.

2. 6 week obedience school [Level I: Basic Obedience Training for Good Home Behavior] taught by Ms. Rix; dog handled by Ms. Brown.

3. Day to day reinforcement and maintenance of training by Ms. Brown.

In October 1988, Ms. Rix flew Keeper to Canine Helpers, inc., in Lockport, N.Y., for specialized handicap training; which included: hearing work and retrieval. After Keeper completed the sixth-month training program our placement agent Ron Edwards arranged several interviews for the dog; and on 5, May 1988 with the approval of Ms. Rix he placed the animal with Himmel House in Rochester NY as an active certified assistance dog.At Himmel House, a group home for the severely handi-capped Keepers major responsibility is to act as a hearing ear dog for a deaf resident, waking him in the morning at the sound of the alarm clock, and alerting him to various auditory signals used around the institution Keeper also serves as a retriever for the other residents who drop things, and are incapable of picking them up.

```
Costs
  Veterinarian                                    $    90
  -includes 2-DHL boosters, rabies
   vaccine, worming, neutering,
   travel certificate

Food                                                   75

Shelter
-Kingdom Kennels                                      125
-foster home (donated by Ms. Brown)                    -

Training
-Kingdom Kennels (donated by Ms. Rix)
-Canine Helpers, Inc.                               1,000

Transportation
-airfare (roundtrip NY)                               230
                                    TOTAL         $1,520
```

5

PROBLEMS WITH OTHER CONVENTIONS

CAPITALIZATION
Capital letters (upper case letters) are used for a variety of purposes. Some rules, such as "Capitalize the first word in a sentence," are easily understood by most writers. Other rules, however, are more difficult to master--with experts far from unanimous in their interpretations of these rules. Therefore, we offer you the forthcoming discussion of frequent areas of confusion in capitalization, with some suggestions for logical usage. Keep in mind that the purpose for adhering to any writing convention is to produce clear prose and that consistency of usage throughout a piece of writing is essential to clarity.

1. **Capitalize proper nouns and adjectives derived from proper nouns.**
   Examine the following examples. They illustrate the differences between specific ("proper") usage, which requires capital letters, and general ("common") usage, which calls for lower-case letters.

   ORGANIZATIONS
   ...including businesses, institutions, associations, etc.

   > **SPECIFIC:** The contract was awarded to Dupre Construction, Inc.

   > **GENERAL:** The contract was awarded to a local construction firm.

   Organizations usually capitalize their department names and other internal divisions.

   > **EXAMPLE:** The Engineering Department is responsible for the design and construction of all projects.

   TITLES
   ...including president, chairman of the board, chief executive officer, senator, mayor, etc.

   > **SPECIFIC:** The sudden retirement of Chairman of the Board Blaylock caused a temporary decline in the value of common stock.

   > **GENERAL:** When a chairman of the board retires suddenly, the value of common stock usually declines.

   GEOGRAPHIC/POLITICAL DIVISIONS
   ...including countries, states, counties, wards, precincts, etc.

   > **SPECIFIC:** Pasco County in Florida has experienced an explosive population growth in the last five years.

GENERAL: The county has experienced an explosive population
growth in the last five years.

GEOGRAPHIC FEATURES
...including rivers, lakes, mountains, gulfs, oceans, etc.

SPECIFIC: Five water samples were drawn from Tampa Bay last
month.

GENERAL: Five water samples were drawn from the bay last
month.

THOROUGHFARES
...including interstate highways, boulevards, avenues, streets,
roads, canals, channels, etc.

SPECIFIC: The proposed construction site is on the southeast
corner of Edison and Orleans Avenues.
GENERAL: The proposed construction site is on the south
side of the avenue.

DIRECTIONS (in terms of location):
...including north, south, east, west, midwest, northeast, etc.

SPECIFIC: The majority of the survey responses came from
the Midwest.

GENERAL: The majority of the survey responses came from the
midwestern states.

2. **Capitalize abbreviations, initialisms, and acronyms when the words they replace would require capital letters.**

EXAMPLE: The Center for Interactive Technology,
Applications, and Research (CITAR) is a
grant-funded organization.

3. **Capitalize the major words in the titles of books, chapters, articles, films, television programs, etc.**

Articles, conjunctions, and prepositions of fewer than five letters
are not capitalized unless they are the first or last words in the
title.

EXAMPLE: Our corporation is sponsoring the production of a
documentary, <u>Survival in the Outback.</u>

EXAMPLE: J. Nelson's article, "An Economy Under Siege,"
examines the 1988 closing of Panamanian banks.

Capitalize subtitles exactly as you would primary titles,
separating the two titles with a colon.

EXAMPLE: "Pine Key Deer: The Ecological Balance" appears in the latest issue of <u>The Florida Journal of Science.</u>

4. **Capitalize major divisions of certain units when they appear with numbers or letters.**

Some major divisions include chapters of books, names of standardized forms, room or suite numbers. **Do not** capitalize minor divisions, such as page and line number.

EXAMPLES: ...Chapter 2, page 10....

...Form B, line 3....

5. **Capitalize the first word of a complete sentence that follows a colon.**

EXAMPLE: The efficiency rating for the assembly line was low: It received a score of only 47 out of a possible 100.

Some handbooks and textbooks suggest that this convention is optional, unless the sentence happens to be a direct quotation, in which case the first letter must be capitalized. We remind you, however, to maintain consistency.

Do not capitalize the first word after a colon if the elements do not constitute a complete sentence (unless another capitalization rule applies.)

EXAMPLE: The report lacked one essential characteristic: objectivity.

6. **When referring to biological classifications, capitalize the genus of an organism but not the name of the species. (The Latin terms are italicized.)**

EXAMPLE: The bufflehead, <u>Bucephala</u> <u>albeola</u>, is a small North American duck with black and white plumage.

NUMBERS

Because numbers can be expressed as either words or figures, occasionally you may be unsure which form to use. Generally, use **words** for whole numbers between zero and ten; use **figures** for numbers greater than ten.

Unfortunately, as with many other language conventions, **there are several exceptions to the rule.**

1. Never begin a sentence with a figure; always spell out the word(s).

INCORRECT: 15 associates attended the conference in Orlando.

CORRECT: Fifteen associates attended the conference in Orlando.

2. **When two numbers occur adjacently in a phrase, use figures for one and write out the word(s) for the other.**

   INCORRECT: This package contains 10 5-barreled hinges.

   CORRECT: This package contains ten 5-barreled hinges.

   or

   This package contains 10 five-barreled hinges.

3. **If the appearance of numbers in your text is frequent, use figures throughout to facilitate readability.**

   EXAMPLE: The attorney's itemized statement shows charges for 15 interstate telephone calls and 3 intercontinental cablegrams.

4. **When two or more numbers (non-adjacent) occur in the same sentence or paragraph, their mode of expression must be consistent.**

   EXAMPLE: The fleet order from Wycott Industries consisted of 5 sedans, 15 panel vans, and 10 pick-up trucks.

5. **For use of hyphens with numbers, both words and figures, see the section on hyphens in Chapter 4.**

6. **Use figures to identify and refer to tables and figures (charts, graphs, and illustrations).**

   EXAMPLES: Table 1
   Figure 3

EXERCISE 1
MASTERING CAPITALS/NUMBERS

DIRECTIONS: The following sentences may contain errors in capitalization and in the expression of numbers. Identify the problems and re write the sentences correctly.

1. Formed by the junction of the Chattahoochee and Flint rivers, the Apalachicola river flows from Southwestern georgia through North western Florida.

2. In the last six months, John Redner has missed ten days of work, and he was 25 minutes late for a meeting with his supervisor.

3. Hydrochloric and Sulfuric acids, when dissolved in water, completely dissociate into ions.

4. Several items are on back-order: 6 2-inch regulators, 10 $\frac{1}{4}$-inch needle valves, and 10 4-inch valve plugs.

5. Please reread Page 14 of the contract and initial Lines three, eight, and 12, which reflect the most recent ch nges in wording.

6. Thomas Hix, the Comptroller, initiated the audit of the operations department.

7. The local chapter of our Labor Union voted to strike if Management refuses to increase hourly wages.

8. Some offshore oil wells are located as far as ninety miles out in the Gulf, are drilled in 350 feet of water, and frequently reach a depth of three miles.

9. The Safety Officer is responsible for completing Form SP-111 at the end of each month.

10. We expect the equipment to be delivered to our Anderson Road Warehouse by eleven o'clock.

11. Refer to figure 3 for an exploded view of the ball joint.

12. The reason for Smith's dismissal was obvious: His absenteeism.

13. Only four of fifteen chapters for the new safety manual are complete.

14. Safety: its your responsibility, our plant's new safety manual, addresses both indoor and outdoor safety precautions and emergency procedures.

15. Our landscape maintenance contract with greenshadow corp. includes replacement of unhealthy plants.

EXERCISE 2
MASTERING CAPITALIZATION/NUMBERS

DIRECTIONS: Identify and correct the errors in capitalization and the problems with expression of numbers.

The Mud Puppy, also known as the Water Dog, is the common name for several species of aquatic salamander. These various species constitute the genus <u>Necturus</u>. The animals are plentiful in the shallows of lakes, rivers, and streams in the Eastern and Central United States. A full-grown Mud Puppy can attain a length of approximately two feet. Ominous-looking with its rectangular, flat head and its dark brown, slimy body, which sports three pairs of conspicuous bushy gills for underwater breathing, the salamander is actually mild-mannered. Sluggish, it spends most of the day in the mud feeding on fish eggs, insect larvae, aquatic worms, and some shellfish. In Spring, the female lays between 60 and 70 eggs in shallow water. A newly hatched Mud Puppy measures about three-quarters of an inch. Mud Puppies are useful to man because of the information they provide to Science.

APPENDICES

A. Selected Documentation Styles

B. Manuscript Preparation Guide

C. Selected List of Word Processing Packages

APPENDIX A: SELECTED DOCUMENTATION STYLES

DOCUMENTATION
There are several documentation styles available for your use when drafting a document. The rule of thumb is to use the style acceptable to your discipline. Included here is a style used most frequently in the technical field. We include here examples of areas we've found to give writers most trouble. For a detailed discussion of each format mentioned here, check with the source itself. A list of styles and their addresses appears at the end of this section.

THE NAME AND YEAR SYSTEM OF DOCUMENTATION
This system is recommended by the American Psychological Association **(APA).** It is recommended for reports from the following disciplines: biological and earth sciences, business, education, and social sciences. With this system of **in-text citation** is recommended a list of references following the report. The following are guidelines for use:

> 1. **If you mention the author's name in the sentence, immediately after the name cite in parentheses the publication year of the source.**

EXAMPLE:

Duke's **(1974)** survey of composition requirements of a random sample of 700 four-year colleges and universities indicated that the majority required two semesters of composition.

> 2. **In places where you do not mention the author's name in the sentence, cite in parentheses the author's last name and the year of the source.**

EXAMPLE:

In a survey of composition requirements of a random sample of 700 four-year colleges and universities **(Duke, 1974),** the responses indicated that the majority required two semesters of composition.

> 3. **If you include in the sentence the author's name and the year of the source, parentheses are <u>not</u> necessary; just separate the date and name with a comma.**

EXAMPLE:

In **1974, Duke** conducted a survey of composition requirements of a random sample of 700 four-year colleges and universities and found that the majority required two semesters of composition.

NOTE:

1. If the source is authored by two, use both authors' names: **(Duke & Bryant, 1974)** or **In 1974, Duke and Bryant....**

2. If the source has three to five authors, use all names the first time you make reference to the source: **(Duke, Bryant, Green, Smith, & Jones, 1974)**. After that, refer to the source as **(Duke, et al., 1974)**.

3. For six or more authors, use **(Duke, et al., 1974)**.

4. If the source is authored by an association, organization, or agency, use its name as the author.

   EXAMPLE:

   Tampa Chamber of Commerce (1982)

5. If no author is listed as the source, use the title of the source and the year.

   EXAMPLE:

   {BOOK}
   Examples were extracted from <u>Handbook of Technical Communication</u> (1988).

   {ARTICLE}
   Examples were extracted from "Tips for the Technician" (1988) to illustrate the samples.

6. Cite an anonymous author as "Anonymous."

   EXAMPLE:

   (Anonymous, 1988)

7. If you are using a source by two or more authors with the same last name, use each author's initials in <u>all</u> citations.

   EXAMPLE:

   J. E. Duke (1974) and A. L. Duke (1981) discovered several responses.

8. If you are not referring to the author's <u>entire</u> work, but to a specific part of the work, cite the part.

   EXAMPLE:

   (Duke, 1974, chap. 5)   {A specific chapter}

   (Duke, 1974, p. 99)   {A specific page}

9. If you make reference to a letter, a memo, a conversation,

etc., use **"personal communication"** as the source.

EXAMPLE:

Abrams (personal communication, March 10, 1988)

or

(T. Abrams, personal communication, March 10, 1988)

10. If you make reference to a court case, cite the name of the case, followed by the decision year.

EXAMPLE:

Brown v. Brown (1954)

or
(Brown v. Brown, 1954)

10. If you make reference to a statute, cite the name of the statute and the year of the enactment.

EXAMPLE:

National Labor Relations Act (1935)

or

National Labor Relations Act of 1935

Specific guidelines govern the manner in which you document direct quotations. For a direct quotation:

1. Cite the source.

2. Place the author, year, and page number in parentheses.

NOTICE the placement of punctuation marks in the following examples.

EXAMPLE 1 - She stated, "This data does not demonstrate a significant change" (Duke, 1984, p. 310), but plans have been implemented to upgrade the program.

EXAMPLE 2 - Considerably more growth was found in the subjects' verbal abilities, but there was little evidence that they improved their writing style" (Bryant et al., 1982, p. 20).

PAY PARTICULAR ATTENTION TO THE EXAMPLE THAT FOLLOWS. THIS IS AN EXAMPLE OF A LONG QUOTATION.

EXAMPLE 3 -

Bryant (1976) found the following:

> The students of the high ability level did not gain significantly more than the students of the low ability level. That they failed to improve significantly in writing proficiency led the investigator to draw several conclusions which might have contributed to the lack of significant improvement. These conclusions suggest several research questions for which careful sought out answers might prove helpful to persons who use the data revealed by the testing instrument. (p. 140)

REFERENCE LIST
The reference list (placed at the end of your document) should cite only sources that you used in the research and preparation of your document. The following guidelines should help you.

1. Alphabetize the list by the last name of the <u>first</u> author of each entry.

2. Double-space each entry.

3. Place single-author entries before multiple- author entries that begin with the same last name.

   Duke, J. A. (1976)

   Duke, J. A., & Bryant, A. G. (1978)

4. Alphabetize by the last name of the second author if you have references with the same first author and different second author.

   Duke J. A., & Abrams (1976)

   Duke, J. A., Bryant, A. G. (1978)

5. Alphabetize by year of publication, references to the same authors of multiple works. (List the earliest work first.)

   Duke, J. A., & Bryant, A. G. (1976)

   Duke, J. A., & Bryant A. G. (1988)

The following examples illustrate sample entries for reference lists. Refer to these examples when in doubt about format of a specific entry type.

EXAMPLES OF REFERENCES TO PERIODICALS

1. Journal article with one author

Astin, A. (1965). The environmental assessment technique: A way to measure college environments. _Journal of Educational Psychology_, _52_, 308-316.

2. Journal article with two authors from a journal paginated by issue

Hunt, D. E., & Hardt, R. H. (1969). The effect of upward programs on the attitudes, motivation and academic achievement of Negro students. _Journal of Social Issues_, _25_, 117-130.

3. Journal article with more than two authors

Bergen, G. R., Upham, J. A., & Bergen, M. B. (1970). Do scholarships affect academic achievement? _Journal of College Student Personnel_, _11_, 383-384.

4. Journal article with six or more authors

Duke, J. A., Bryant, A. G., Abrams, T., Ross, W., Metzger, E., & Heim, W. (1987). The efffects of ultraviolet rays on the skin. _Journal of Scientific Discovery_, _7_, 691-794.

5. Magazine article entry

Brown, L. D. (1978, January). Can we survive this year? _Life_, pp. 29-31.

6. Newsletter article with a corporate author

Staff. (1988, August 29). Technical application of databases. _Today's Technology_, p. 20.

7. Newspaper article with no author

Big mac attacks to protest McPrefix. (1988, April 25). _The Tampa Tribune_, p. 1D.

8. Newspaper article with discontinuous pages

Shelton, B. (1988, April 25). Printer hopes other women follow entrepreneurial path. _The Tampa Tribune_, pp. 1D, 4D.

9. Newspaper article (letter to editor)

   Bland, J. (1981, January 1). Help save the city [Letter to the
   editor]. The Tampa Tribune, p. 3.

10. Edition other than first by an author with "Jr." in name

   Hayes, T., Jr., & Hayes, J. (1981). What it takes to win
   (3rd ed.). New York: Prentice Hall.

11. Entry when author and publisher are the same and the author is an
   agency or organization.

   National Council of Technicians. (1988). Technical manual for
   type-two printers (3rd ed.). Bloomington, Indiana: Author.

12. Book that is edited

   Duke, J. A., & Bryant, A. G. (Eds.). (1988). Technical
   education in the schools. New York: Oxford.

13. Revised edition of a book

   Farrell, J. (1987). Technical functions of compressors (rev.
   ed.). Atlanta: Harcourt Brace Jovanovich.

14. Two-author article of chapter in an edited book

   Peters, A., & Peters, C. (1985). Planning family outings. In
   J. A. Duke, & A. G. Bryant (Eds.), Technical education in the
   schools (pp. 121-125). Atlanta: Harcourt Brace Jovanovich.

15. Report from a corporate organization

   National Science Foundation. (1980). Special report on scientific projects (Publication No. 25-8701). Washington, D.C.:
   U. S. Government Printing Office.

16. Report from a private organization

   Tampa Urban League. (1976). Needs of the communities (Research
   Rep. No. 736). Tampa, FL: Author.

17. Film entry

   Duke, J. A. (Producer), & Bryant, A. G. (Director). (1984).

   <u>Preparing for the personal interview</u> [Film]. Dubuque, IA:

   Kendall/Hunt.

18. Computer program

   IBM (1987). <u>Displaywrite 4</u> [Computer program]. Boca Raton, FL:

   Author.

STYLE MANUALS

American Mathematical Society. (1980). A manual for authors of mathematical papers (7th ed.). Providence, RI: Author.

American Psychological Association. (1983). Publication manual of the American Psychological Association (3rd ed.). Washington, DC: Author.

Brusaw, C. T., Alred, G. J., & Oliu, W. E. (1987). The business writer's handbook (3rd ed.). New York: St. Martin's Press.

Brusaw, C.T., Alred, G. J., & Oliu, W. E. (1987). Handbook of technical writing (3rd ed.). New York: St. Martin's Press.

Chicago guide to preparing electronic manuscripts. (1987). Chicago: The University of Chicago Press.

Council of Biology Editors, Style Manuals Committee. (1983). CBE style manual: A guide for authors, editors, and publishers in the biological sciences (5th ed.). Bethesda: Council of Biology Editors.

House, C. R., & Sigler, K. (1981). Reference manual for office personnel (6th ed.). Cincinnati: South-Western Publishing Company.

Keithley, E. M., Flatley, M. E., & Schreiner, P. J. (1989) [sic]. Manual of style for business letters, memos, & reports. Cincinnati: South-Western Publishing Company.

NOTE: Reprints of "Information for IEEE authors" are available on request from the Editorial Department, Institute of Electrical and Electronics Engineers, Inc., 345 47th Street, New York, NY 10017.

APPENDIX B: MANUSCRIPT PREPARATION GUIDE

Preparing the manuscript format for your report deserves at least as much attention as you afforded the composition of your text. The expression "Appearances count" is especially applicable to technical writing. As a visual complement to the text, headings and illustrations as well as the margins, spacing, typeface, and paper quality you use affect the readability of your manuscript. Therefore, you will want to make your decisions carefully, remembering that clarity is your ultimate goal.

REPORT ELEMENTS

The length of the manuscript and your presentation purpose will help you determine which elements to incorporate into your final report. Standard report elements include the following:

> Cover
> Letter of Transmittal
> Title Page
> Table of Contents
> List of Illustrations
> Acknowledgments
> Executive Summary
> Abstract
> Body
> Works Cited
> Appendixes

Cover. If your report is lengthy, binding it in a cover is a good idea. The cover should be labeled with the title of the report and, if appropriate, the name of the author, the date, the report number, or any other pertinent information. If your cover is transparent, place a blank sheet of paper behind it.

Letter of Transmittal. A letter of transmittal is sent to the recipient of your report to indicate the manner in which the manuscript is being transmitted: either accompanying the letter or under separate cover and either by mail or by courier. (Use a memo to transmit in-house reports.) The content of the letter should be brief, containing the reason for the report and a short summary of the content. If the letter accompanies a bound report, its placement is usually immediately before or immediately following the title page.

Title page. The title page contains two requisite pieces of information--the title of the report and the author's name. Other information, such as the date, the report number, or the recipient of the report, may also appear on this page. Occasionally the format of the title page may be pre-formatted, with the necessary information already determined for you. If you must design your own format, determine which items suit your purpose and arrange them logically, both visually and textually.

Table of Contents. A report of five pages or more should contain a table of contents. Essentially, it is an outline of your report listing the headings (written in parallel language, of course) that appear in the report and their page numbers. The table of contents usually follows the title page.

List of Illustrations. A report with five or more figures or tables should contain a list of illustrations. List the figures and tables under separate headings, identifying each illustration with its respective number, caption, and page number. These lists may directly follow, on the same page, the table of contents or they may appear on a separate page directly following the table of contents.

Acknowledgements. You may want to express your gratitude to those who provided you with assistance, financial or otherwise. This section may be included in the preliminary pages or at the end of the body.

Executive Summary. An executive summary appears at the beginning of the report and is intended for executives whose busy schedules may not allow them to read the entire report. The traditional summary at the end of the body is directed toward readers who have read the entire report.

Abstract. The abstract is a brief summary of key points in the text. The placement of abstracts is acceptable in several locations--on the title page; at the top of page 1; centered above the introduction; or on a separate page immediately preceding the body.

Body. The body of the report contains the core of your text along with any illustrations you have included to enhance your writing. The internal divisions and arrangement of the information will depend on your purpose in creating the report, but they must also be logically and consistently presented.

Works Cited. This section lists the references cited in your text. It may also be titled "References" or "Bibliography." Formats for presenting this list vary among disciplines. Some of the most widely used style sheets include the <u>Turabian</u>, the <u>MLA</u> (Modern Language Association), and the APA (American Psychological Association). (**See APPENDIX A for more information on documentation styles.**) The works cited section immediately follows the body of the report.

Appendices. An appendix contains information that is only peripherally related to the body, such as the information in the appendices of this book. Always title your appendix, and if your report contains more than one appendix, use numbers or letters to identify each one further. The appendix constitutes the final section of your document.

Headings. In technical reports, the information is divided into logical sections and subsections, labeled clearly and accurately. The wording of the headings must be identical to that which appears in the table of contents. In addition, the physical appearance and placement of the headings should reflect the "order" of the heading. For example, the title of the report and the title of an appendix are first-order headings with further divisions being second order, third order, and so on. The breakdown of material does not usually extend beyond a fifth or sixth order. If you produce your final manuscript on a typewriter, you may use centering, capitalization, underlining and indentation to distinguish the various levels of headings. If you have access to a desktop publishing system, however, you can also boldface and italicize to differentiate the levels.

Illustrations. There are two major categories of illustrations: tables and figures. Tables contain numerical data arranged in columns and rows, each of which must be appropriately labeled with a number, which is followed by a caption that further identifies it.

> **EXAMPLE:** Table 1. Water test results.

The label and caption for a table are usually located **above** the table itself.

Figures are any visual aids that are not tables, including charts, graphs, photographs, schematics, and so on. Like tables, all figures must be labeled with a number and a caption.

> **EXAMPLE:** Figure 1. Bunsen burner.

These identifying labels usually appear **below** the figure.

Refer to your illustrations in your writing and place them as closely to their related text as possible. If you borrow or adapt another author's illustration, document the source parenthetically immediately after the caption.

Remember that tables and figures enhance your text; they should not be used as a substitute for clear prose.

Margins. Generally you should maintain margins of one inch on both sides as well as top and bottom. If the document is to be bound, however, you will need to adjust the bound margin to compensate for the cover. Pages on which titles appear should have a top margin of at least two inches.

Spacing. You may choose to single space or double space your manuscript. In lengthy documents that are not subdivided by headings or for reports that will be submitted for publication, you should use the double-space format. However, if the report or the sections are brief, you may want to single space to enhance the readability of your manuscript. When double spacing, either triple or quadruple space between headings. If you single space, then double space between headings and paragraphs.

Preface. When you choose the typeface for your report, you must consider both the size of the type (e.g., 10, 12, or 15 pitch) and the style of the "face." Pica (10 pitch) and elite (12 pitch) are standard on most typewriters and computers. The use of a size smaller than elite to print the document is not generally recommended since it may be difficult to read. (Smaller type, however, may be ideal for labeling illustrations or for producing lower level headings.)

Use traditional typeface (e.g., prestige, boldface, etc., but <u>not</u> script) to print your report. Nontraditional styles may be difficult to read or may distract the reader from the content.

Paper Quality. Use standard 8½" x 11" bond or rag paper; and unless your organization or business firm dictates the use of colored paper, use white. Also avoid submitting reports printed on erasable bond, since handling often causes the type to smear on the page.

APPENDIX C: SELECTED LIST OF WORD PROCESSING PACKAGES

PRODUCT	VENDOR
Display Write	IBM
Lotus Manuscript	Lotus
Microsoft Word	Microsoft
Multimate	Ashton-Tate
PC-Write	Quicksoft
PFS: Professional Writer	Software Production
Student Word Perfect	Word Perfect Corp.
Word Perfect	Word Perfect Corp.
Word Perfect Jr.	Word Perfect Corp.
Wordstar	Micropro International

STYLE CHECKERS

Grammatik	Reference Software
RightWriter	Rightsoft

INDEX